LEAVING HOME!

Practical Stuff to Help You Survive in College and Beyond

ANNI GRIMWADE

Rampallion Press

What Others Are Saying...

"Full of tips you won't find anywhere else. I would definitely recommend it." Emily Drew (19)

"Essential for anyone leaving home. It's a must-have even for those who think they know everything!" William Brookes (21)

"There's not much you need to know when you first move out of home that isn't in this book." Penny Lafferty (25)

"Pack this book along with everything else when you leave home. You'll need it!" Josh Lord (23)

Published by Rampallion Press
Printed in the U.S. by Amazon.com, Inc.
Website: www.rampallionpress.com.au

Copyright © Anni Grimwade 2016
Editing: Daphne Parsekian
Typesetting: Dr Jay Polmar
Cover design: alerrandre & Dr Jay Polmar

Grimwade, Anni
LEAVING HOME!: Practical Stuff to Help You Survive in College and Beyond

ISBN: 978-0-9925928-2-0
Life skills.
Young adults-life skills guides.
646.7

Dedication

Leaving Home is dedicated to all of you who are moving
out of home for the first time.

Don't worry. I've got your back.

Acknowledgments

Thank you to Kristin Hayward, Mike Hutchinson, Merriam Saunders, and Molly Toyne for their practical help and technical advice.

It takes a village to raise a child or write a book, and my village is made up of the following lovely people: Martine Browell, Caroline & Marcus Cottrill, Rhonda and Blair Denys, Niki Dimopoulos, the East Malvern Ladies' Mahjong Club (EMLMC), Fred Grimwade, Joan Grimwade, Lisa Grimwade, Martin Grimwade, Rebecca Imbrosciano, Marianne Kagiaros, Sophie Kempton, Kara Lowe, Samantha Macansh, Daphne Persekian, Julie Postance, Archie Roberts, Hamish Roberts, Hannah Roberts, Tim Roberts, Jenny Thompson, Pru Thompson, WOGBOM, and, of course, Donald Ward.

Thank you all.

About the Author

The short version:

Anni Grimwade is a mom who knows a whole heap of stuff about managing your life when you move out of home. Read up.

The long version:

Anni Grimwade started professional life as a physical therapist before realizing that she was better at management than at treating injured people. After more study in Melbourne and New York, to her relief she ended up with an MBA, whereupon she moved to Hong Kong. She worked as the general manager of a recruitment company and subsequently as a professor before the handover of the colony to Chinese rule in 1997.

During a five-year stay in Jakarta, Anni undertook freelance editing work and then moved to Australia with a growing family, where she has undertaken a range of management consulting assignments.

Throughout these different careers, she has baked furiously, qualified as a wedding cake decorator, opened a holiday sewing school for teenagers, become the spreadsheet queen of budgeting for family and friends, and cleaned her house begrudgingly. She is quite good at French, not too bad at Indonesian, and tries her hand at speaking Teenager as well.

Anni lives with her husband Tim and three teenage children, none of whom listen to her. She will give them each a copy of this book.

Contents

Introduction

Do you feel like you are on the brink of a huge adventure? You are! You are moving out of home — maybe to college — and it is the beginning of a new and independent phase of your life.

Don't stress out — this book will give you all the practical skills you need to help you survive. It will help you stay healthy, manage your money, take care of your clothes and the rest of your stuff, buy and look after a car, get a good job, and handle an emergency.

Have fun! Conquer the world! But like your mom says, look after yourself along the way.

Anni Grimwade
April 2016

CHAPTER 1

Serious Money Stuff

W hen it comes to money, it's the little things that can make a difference. Ever heard the saying "Beware of little expenses; a small leak will sink a big ship"? (Yep, it was Benjamin Franklin who said it.) It's true: Be careful with all your small money decisions, and you'll end up sitting on a pile of gold coins, metaphorically speaking.

So to make sure you and your money continue to have a harmonious relationship, read on. It could save you from lots of grief (and the truly horrible prospect of having to ask your parents for money — again).

Haven't Got Time to Read the Whole Chapter? Read This.

1. A budget is important. It doesn't matter whether you do it online, use an app, or scribble on a piece of paper, but you need to know where your money's coming from and where it's going when it's heading out that door. A budget helps you work out where you really stand financially.

2. Practice good money habits. Frugal is the new black. Try to earn as much as possible, spend as little as possible, and save the difference. It's the recipe for financial happiness.

3. When you are shopping online, use a secure payment method such as PayPal. Don't hand over your card details to just anyone online, and be on the lookout for dicey websites. Poor grammar, spelling mistakes, blurry logos, and requests for too much information are dead giveaways that something's not right.

4. If your phone gets stolen, report it immediately to your cell phone company. You are responsible for any calls, texts, or data downloads on it until you do. And if it's your ATM card that is lost, make sure you let your bank know immediately, and then check your card statements to make sure no one's going wild on your behalf.

5. If you buy overseas currency before you depart on vacation, you can be hit hard with high fees, either at the bank or at the airport on departure. Withdrawing cash from an ATM at your destination is the way to go.

Budgeting

Okay, I'm not sure you'll like this idea, but one of the first things you need to do when you move out of home is set up a budget. This is a list of all the income you receive (such as salary, allowances, huge monetary gifts from your fabulously wealthy special friend, or other payments) compared to a total of all the expenses you have (such as those associated with your new dope lifestyle, going out, your car, new clothes etc.). A budget will cover one full year of income and expenses, which usually covers a calendar year from the 1st of January to the 31st of December.

Why are budgets so important?

A budget is important because it tells you where your hard-earned money is going, stops you from spending more than you are earning, and helps you think about where you might need to cut back. It gives you an idea of what your financial position really is, not just what it feels like, and it helps you in forming realistic financial goals, both short-term (saving for that fabulous new pair of skis) and long-term (saving for a down payment on a house).

When you first put together a budget, it will become clear how important it is to keep good records. A very simple and low-tech method is to put all your receipts and statements into a shoebox as they come in. These can include payslips, phone bills, doctors' receipts, electricity statements, insurance statements, love letters, etc. (No, not really love letters — I just wrote that to check that you were awake). Until you manage to have a full year of all these papers and while you do your first budget, you will need to "guestimate" some of the totals. A really easy way to keep a record of your spending is to use an app — there are millions out there, but if you don't have time to look around, look at *Dollarbird* or *Spendee*. These are just two, but they work well and are simple to use so are as good a place to start as any.

A budget is important

How do I do a budget?

It doesn't matter how you set up your budget, although using a computer spreadsheet means you can personalize it to your exact circumstances. It will do all your calculations for you and each year you can save annual copies, which can help you see how your financial position is changing. (Hopefully better and better.)

A really excellent alternative is an app such as *Budgt* — maybe the best 99 cents you'll spend at the App Store. It is easy to use and will painlessly manage your budget with minimal effort. Most banks also have a budgeting tool on their websites, so go online and look around.

But if this sounds too serious, even a piece of paper can give you a good start.

Sample budget

If you're a pen and paper type of person, here's a sample budget to photocopy and fill in. (I'm sure your mom told you not to write in books!)

MY BUDGET		For the year ending:_____	
		Monthly	Annual
Income			
	Salary		
	Allowance		
	Other Payments		
TOTAL		$	$

Expenses			
Household	Rent		
	Food		
	Eating out		
	Insurance		
	Electricity		
	Gas		
	Water		
	Repairs		
	Home phone		
	Cell phone		
	Internet		

Education	Tuition fees		
	Books		
	Other Education Expenses		
Social	Going out		
	Gifts		
	Clubs or subscriptions		
Car	Loan repayments		
	Registration		
	Insurance		
	Gas		
	Repairs		
	Automobile association		
	Electronic tolls		
	Parking		
	Cleaning		
Other Transport	Public transportation tickets		
	Bike maintenance		
Clothes	New clothes		
	New shoes		
	Dry cleaning		
	Clothing repairs		

Health	Doctor		
	Health insurance		
	Dentist		
	Drug store		
	Physical therapist		
	Hairdresser, spa		
Pets	Food		
	Registration		
	Vet		
Other	Investment/savings		
	Retirement fund		
	Donations		
	Travel savings		
	Holiday savings		
	Emergency/contingency		
TOTAL		$	$

How to manage a budget

The aim of a budget is to end up with a bottom line that is "in the black" — that is, ending up with money left over from an income that is greater than what you spend. If you find you have a negative bottom line and are "in the red" (spending more than you earn), you will need to do

Budgets need attention

one of two things: either stop eating (well, trim off some of your costs) or earn more income. Usually it's easier to spend less than to earn more, for instance, decreasing the number of restaurant meals you eat rather than getting another part-time job.

You'll need to keep coming back to your budget. Don't think you are bad at managing money if it doesn't work out the first time — budgets need attention ! They stop you from running off the financial rails completely and will allow you to plan for rewards such as vacations, a car, and, ultimately, a down payment for your own house.

What do you do if you are broke?

If you've got delinquent notices pouring through your mailbox, be brave and face the situation. You are not alone and do not need to be embarrassed. Most people have financial stress at some stage in their lives.

- If you can, get advice from a free or subsidized financial counselor. If you are at college, there may be one at Student Services.

- Check with your employer too as many larger companies have Employee Assistance Program (EAP) counselors available for employees at no cost. Talk to them about what options are available to you. And don't worry — it will be confidential.

- How about doing some part-time work around the neighborhood? Offer to babysit for those family friends down the road, or do some gardening for your elderly neighbor.

- To give you some breathing space, call your utility companies (e.g., for electricity, gas, and phone) and tell them that you want to pay their account but are not in a position to do so at the moment. Often they would rather set up a small monthly payment plan than to think you won't pay at all. And it will stop the scary letters.

- For the short term, can you sell something from around the house? An unused piece of gym equipment? Your old textbooks or some DVDs? How about the bike or sewing machine you never use?

- Talk to your friends — they may know of a part-time job available where they work.

- And while you're talking to them, ask your friends for the support that you need. I'm not talking about money here, just a shoulder to cry on or someone to talk to. It won't solve your financial situation, but it will make you feel much better.

Good Money Habits

Okay, remember at the start of this chapter we talked about small leaks sinking big ships? Well, here's the lowdown on how to manage your money at the micro level. All these habits will help you keep your budget in the black, so pay attention — there are 52 of them, so why not try one a week?

Getting more into your wallet...

1. Sell unwanted items on *eBay* or *craigslist*. It's so simple even your parents could do it, and you might be surprised at what you can earn. Try books, and clothes with well-known brand names to start with.

2. Get a part-time job — check out a few relevant websites, or keep an eye out for notices in windows of stores you frequent.

3. Apply for scholarships — lots of them! People in the know have told me that not all scholarships get awarded as they don't always have applications. So apply away — you never know, you could get lucky!

4. Offer to do something for friends that you do well (like cleaning their car or ironing). Even if you don't actually get any cash, you can barter for something they can do better than you (like tutoring you in chemistry or doing a budget).

5. Volunteer to help out at your university or to be a new student guide. You may be given vouchers for the bookstore or get a free lunch.

...and taking less out of it

6. Check what subsidized services are available at your campus or workplace. Think general health, counseling, and study skill seminars.

7. Do you really need to buy that item? If it's not something you will use a lot, see if you can borrow it (e.g., DVDs from friends, books from the library, tools and cooking utensils from neighbors).

8. When you're out shopping, tell yourself you can have that irresistible book, pair of shoes, or piece of sporting equipment — just not today. Wait a couple of days to see if you might actually be able to live without it.

9. Make gifts for your family and friends. Making a cake can take only 10 minutes (plus cooking time), and it's much more meaningful than something you picked up in a rush at the gas station.

10. Try to keep yourself healthy by eating well and exercising, therefore avoiding drug store and other healthcare costs.

11. When you finally get into your own house, think about not having a home phone. It's old technology, and getting rid of it could save you hundreds of dollars a year.

12. Campus clubs or groups can offer all sorts of discounts — on food, trips, coffee, books, performances, printing, and more. Find out what they offer, and then join - even if it's just to get the discounts.

Eating on the cheap

13. Make sure you know what is in your fridge and try to plan your meals so you use everything you have. Be creative, and don't let food go bad.

14. And now that you know what's in your fridge, make a list and stick to it when you're at the store.

15. NEVER buy bottled water if you can drink the local tap water. Never. Refill a bottle, and take it with you. It's like throwing money down the drain if you buy water, and all those bottles will end up in a landfill.

16. Pretend you're a kid again, and take a bag lunch to school or the office. You can save $2,000 a year.

17. Think about not buying coffee when you're out. (Relax — I only said think about it.)

18. Cook at home, and avoid eating in restaurants. For example, don't get into the habit of routinely eating out on Friday nights. Make it "soup night" or "shake the freezer and see what falls out" night.

19. Buy non-perishables such as toilet paper and detergent in bulk if you can afford to and have the storage space.

Avoid buying bottled water

Cheap textbooks

20. Check with students who did the course last year about how much they used the prescribed textbooks. If it's not a lot, you can just borrow them from the library as required.

21. See if you can find out as soon as you enroll what your assigned textbooks will be. Try to source used copies right away – the early bird catching the worm and all that...

22. Use the textbooks that are held on reference in the library. You can only use them for an hour or so, but this means you will actually sit down and do the work, which can be very good for your discipline!

23. Sell your books at the start of the following year. Just before you get back to college, list them so that you get all the "early birds" (see above).

Other ways to be frugal at college

24. Weird but true: Sometimes grocery store school supplies are cheaper than those at the campus store. Check it out.

25. At the end of the school year, go through all your supplies, and keep whatever you can

use the following year. Rip out pages from partly-used lecture pads, empty out folders, and get together pens, pencils, etc. Start the new year a step ahead.

26. If you can wait till the last couple of days before you go to college, buy your supplies then. The closer you get to the start of school, the cheaper it gets.

27. Struggling in one of your subjects — or all of them? Tutors will blow your budget so try online first. *YouTube* and *iTunes U* are two good places to start.

Being frugal at home

28. Make sure you turn lights off when you leave a room. It's better for the environment and you'll save a few pennies too.

29. For the same reasons, put on or take off clothes instead of using heaters and air-conditioners, shut windows and curtains, and use draft stoppers to avoid the need for air-conditioning and heating.

30. Buy any household items that you need at thrift stores, but only buy electrical goods if they have a "safe to use" tag.

31. If you want to buy something new, always check its price on the Internet first. You can then approach your retailer and offer them the chance to sell it to you at the same price or less.

Dressing up for less

32. Buy your clothes from thrift stores. Celebrate your individuality — apart from the cost, an added benefit is that no one will be wearing what you are!

33. Buy formal wear from eBay. Most items have only been worn once or twice, and you can save hundreds of dollars.

34. Get into the habit of offering clothes you are tired of to your friends, and accept their offerings in return. This works well if you can find a friend with similar taste who is a similar size to you.

35. Avoid buying *dry clean only* clothes. It's expensive, and it's a hassle to take them there and pick them up. And have you ever thought about all those weird chemicals next to your skin? Check the care tags before you purchase.

Avoid buying *dry clean only* clothes

36. Learn how to hem and repair your clothes. Look in *Clothing Care 101* (Chapter 7 of this book), or even get onto *YouTube*. It can teach you everything you want to know (and a whole bunch you don't).

Entertainment on the cheap

37. Instead of going out for dinner, have your friends over for a "potluck" meal — everyone brings their own drinks and food to share.

38. Look out for free events such as concerts in the park and festivals, particularly in spring and summer. Your local area will have a program on their website.

39. Don't be pressured into spending to keep up with the people you socialize with — good friends will understand if you have limited funds, and if they don't, perhaps you shouldn't be hanging out with them.

Getting out and about without spending too much

40. Get into the habit of walking, running, or riding your bike. You know it's good for you, good for the environment, and it saves money.

41. Cars are expensive. If you add up the purchase price, repairs, gas, insurance, and registration, you'll be amazed. Maybe public transportation might work for you?

42. If your car needs repairs, don't just get it done at the dealer. Call around to find the cheapest option. And make sure you check in your car manual when your car needs to be serviced, and don't just go by what the mechanic tells you. It can be less often than they recommend.

43. Use cruise control to avoid getting speeding tickets.

44. Remember how much fun it was when you carpooled your way to basketball with all the kids in the back and Mom up front? Relive your youth — see if you can arrange permanent car pools for regular activities.

45. And for occasional trips, see if you can grab a lift this time with someone going your way. Even if you don't have a car, as long as you have a license, you can offer them a lift next time. Check out a car share system such as *Zipcar* or *Car2Go*.

46. Need to get home for the break but want to save the cost of the trip? Look at relocating a rental car or campervan. This can be as cheap as $1 a day, and sometimes they even kick in for gas. Google *car relocation*.

Cheaper money

47. Save up for items that you can't borrow, instead of putting the purchase on your credit card or borrowing the money from the bank.

48. But if you need to take out a loan, make sure you are ruthless in finding the best interest rate. Banks make money by loaning you money and charging you interest, so they all want your business!

49. Get over your embarrassment, and always ask for a discount wherever you shop. And be aware of any discounts you are entitled to at your place of work. Maybe your employer can get you discounts at particular stores or give you cheaper insurance?

50. Be on top of what you can get with your bank card (e.g., travel insurance if you pay for your airfare by credit card)

51. Go for paperless statements, and save the cost of having one sent to you each month.

> **Always ask for a discount wherever you shop**

And one last thing...

52. Don't smoke (you know all the reasons why). If you can't give it up, cut back.

Case Study:

Getting Your Budget into the Black

Matthew did a first draft of his budget and to his horror found that he was spending $2,300 more than he was earning each year. He knew this couldn't continue, so he had a chat with his friends and thought hard about how he could earn more money and spend less.

He knew his neighbor's son was sports crazy and they had an issue with childcare, so being a bit of a basketball legend himself, he offered to look after the son and play sports with him during the semester for a couple of hours a week. She was happy to pay him $30 each time, which gave him $960 a year. He set up an eBay account and started selling DVDs and books, getting about $30 a month ($360 a year), he began taking his lunch to school three days a week saving $30 a week (or $1,560 a year), and he made homemade pizzas every Sunday night instead of ordering take-out ($1,040 a year).

He also finally learned to use the coffee machine at college and twice a week made a coffee there rather than buying one (saving $400 a year). These five small changes meant that when he added up his extra earnings and savings, he was pleased to see that he'd added $4,320 a year to the bottom line and was $2,020 in the black. He could finally afford that vacation to Hawaii.

Lesson: Small weekly changes can make a big difference to your budget.

Shopping Online

Shopping online is one of the joys of life but can be tricky (like your love life). Here are a few tips to help you have smooth sailing:

- When you are shopping online, use a secure payment method such as PayPal. It is not difficult to set up an account – all you need is an email address and a credit or debit card. Once set up, it means that when you buy something from a website, you only hand over your email address and not your credit card details. Avoid making payments by transfers or direct debit.

- Whenever you are making a payment, make sure that you look for the little padlock next to the URL and the letters HTTPS:// rather than just HTTP://. That little S makes all the difference – it means the site has SSL (Secure Sockets Layer) and that your payment is secure.

- Use familiar websites, and be critical of things that look odd. That spelling mistake or dicey logo probably mean that it's a fake website.

- Check that the company has a street address on the website.

- Don't use free Wi-Fi in public areas to do your banking or online shopping. It is not secure.

- Check your statements to see that you've only bought what you wanted to buy.

- Don't give out too much information. For instance, if you feel there is no need to provide your address but the website demands it, enter in "unwilling to divulge address" as the street name and then your zip code. If you need to provide a phone number but you don't want to, enter (555) 900-0000. And if they want your birthday, enter 01/01 of your birth year.

- Never answer emails asking for more information or start dealing with a seller by email — information should only be provided through a website.

- Be careful about add-ons to the cost of anything you are buying, such as postage, packaging and taxes.

- Always check the terms and conditions of any transaction, and either print out a copy, save a .pdf, or take a screen shot for your records.

- If it looks too good to be true, it probably is. There are some great websites out there to check whether the email you've got is legit or not, one of which is *Scamwatch*[1]. While it's not a U.S. site, these scams are pretty universal and travel around the globe faster than a speeding bullet, so the scams we are encountering here will be listed there too.

- Make sure your anti-viral software is up to date.

- And finally, at the end of the day, turn off your computer so potential hackers don't have unimpeded access.

Make sure your anti-viral software is up to date

Traveling Overseas

You've slaved for months to earn enough moolah to go overseas, so the last thing you want is to be separated from your money on the way. There are a few things to remember.

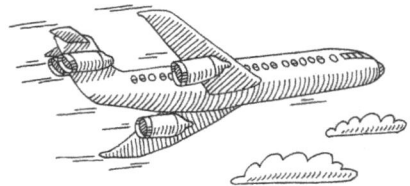

Travel insurance on your credit card

Check it out with the bank first, but often if you pay for your air ticket on your credit card, it will automatically give you travel insurance. This means that if you need to cancel because of illness or you lose your baggage in Barcelona, you are covered. Just make sure that you have the cash ready to pay the credit card account in the first month; otherwise, you'll be paying interest from now till the cows (and you) come home.

Accessing cash

Don't take the currency of your destination with you – get it at the airport as you arrive via your ATM card. You will pay a small fee to your own bank (less than $10), but the withdrawal fee will be more than offset by the better exchange rate you'll get. Make sure you don't take out small amounts each time – take out a large-ish amount (say more than $100) and store most of it in your money belt. Don't do this if you are going to find the nearest bar and spend it all in one night. Duh!

Don't be tempted to exchange money at the airport at a foreign exchange office. They will either have huge fees or a really poor rate – and sometimes both.

Another way to take your money is to take a travel card with you that is pre-loaded in the currency of your choice. Personally, I find this a hassle, and you should be aware that large fees can be attached to their use. On the other hand though (and I like to be fair), these cards can be good if you plan to stay in dicey places where the card might find its way into someone else's pocket. Those slimy thieves will then only be able to access the money on that card, not all the money in your account. If you choose to take a travel card, shop around for one with the best rates and fees.

Keeping it safe

If you are traveling with someone trustworthy, split your valuables. (And if they're not trustworthy, why are you traveling with them?) Give them a card of yours so that if you lose your wallet, all is not lost. Use a money belt to keep most of your valuables in – the ones around your neck are great but can be annoying and rub in hot weather as well as being obvious; some people like the waist ones, but if you are a woman, have you ever tried to access one in a dress? With a money belt storing most of your valuables, you can then use a wallet in your bag or pocket with just a small amount of everyday cash in it.

In terms of insurance, check out your or your parents' normal homeowner's/renter's insurance at home to see if it covers goods being taken overseas, such as your laptop or cell phone. You may be able to itemize them on your policy for as little as $4 a month to cover them while you are away. You can also sometimes insure your phone through your telecommunications provider, but this can be expensive.

Which currency?

When you're away, always pay in local currency — anything you see in dollar prices will be overpriced. And always know the value of your currency.

Always pay in local currency when traveling overseas

Case Study:
Local Currency

Emily is in India and is having a blast at the local market. She finds a groovy little dress for 200 rupees or $10 and decides to pay in dollars because it seems so cheap and she has it handy. Little does she know that the price in rupees is worth just over $3, so she has just paid more than three times as much as she should have.

Lesson: Always know the value of the local currency, and pay in it.

Keeping in touch

Be really, really careful using your phone overseas. For some reason, cell phone companies love to gouge you in any way they can while you are away, and you can be presented with a truly horrible account as a travel souvenir when you get home. You can arrange an international calling plan with your provider before you leave home or, even better, buy a SIM card when you arrive at your destination airport. Depending on what you are after, they can be as little as $20.

Alternatively, you can also use email or local international phone calling cards to keep in contact with your family. Your mother will be going bananas if you don't contact her, so put her out of her misery. But do it cheaply.

Give away those coins

Coins are useless outside their own country and can't be changed back at home, so either buy a drink or something cheap just before you leave to come back home or, even better, put them in the UNICEF envelope on the plane. Lighten your wallet AND get good karma too!

Checklist: Getting good value when you travel

✔ Don't spend your precious money on water — if you're in a country where the water is potable (meaning able to be drunk, not able to be put in a pot!), make sure you always ask for tap water rather than buying the bottled stuff. You'll save tons.

✔ If you are in a country with a different language, don't eat or drink at places that have big signs in English. You can bet that these are tourist traps and will cost you big time. Enjoy picnics with food from supermarkets or local stores.

✔ Eat up big at that breakfast buffet. In theory, it might prevent you from having to buy lunch (although it doesn't work for me).

✔ Unless it's for safety reasons, use the public transportation system. It's the way the locals go, so you'll see more of the local life than if you are stuck in a cab.

✔ Travel in the off-season: If you are traveling at home or in Europe, this will mean traveling outside June to September, and in Asia, it means traveling in the rainy or hot seasons. This makes it much cheaper, but there are reasons they are the off-season — usually climatic.

✔ Do your research before you go, both on the 'net and by taking guidebooks with you. Don't spend a fortune on your travel and then be stingy with your travel guidebook — just one or two really good tips can save you the cost of the book.

✔ Look at booking some things before you leave. For instance, making a reservation for a trip up the Eiffel Tower can save you four hours of queuing — and who wants to spend a precious day in Paris in a line?

Five Top Tips

1. Save up instead of borrowing but if you do have to take out a loan, get the lowest interest rate you can and pay it off as quickly as you can.

2. Keep on top of things financially by: increasing your income, spending less on non-essentials, eating frugally, being economical at home and not smoking. Ever.

3. You can tell if a website is secure by checking if there is a little padlock next to the URL and there are the letters HTTPS rather than just HTTP. But I bet you knew that.

4. If you are broke, seek help early. Take a deep breath and act before it gets even more out of control.

5. If you travel overseas, buy a SIM card at your destination to make calls and send texts. You'll be hit hard if you don't.

CHAPTER 2

A Place to Call Home

I f you're moving onto your college campus, then you're off the hook! Skip this chapter for a couple of years, and come back to read it then. But at some stage. you'll move out into your very own place, and unless Great-aunt Peggy has left you a fortune or you were a teenage dotcom billionaire, you will probably have to rent your first home and find some roommates when you do. You will be thinking about how great it will be to finally be out on your own, but there are a few things to remember, so read on.

Haven't Got Time to Read the Whole Chapter? Read This.

1. Moving out is expensive! In addition to the rent, add up the cost of the security deposit, moving expenses, furniture, and utilities, and be amazed.

2. A rental agreement is a legal contract. Once you sign it, you can't change your mind.

3. Choose your roommate carefully. Make sure you know them well and have similar lifestyles.

4. Establish the ground rules early on. At a minimum, work out how you will share money, cleaning, and food.

5. Get your own insurance — the landlord (owner) won't cover your computer or other valuables, even if there's a leak from upstairs.

Can You Afford to Move Out?

Moving out can be expensive. It's not just the monthly cost of renting your dream home; there are a lot of other expenses as well. Make sure you consider these costs:

- The security deposit (this can be equivalent to up to two months' rent)
- Moving fees (or thank you pizzas if friends are helping)
- Furniture
- Kitchen utensils, dinnerware & silverware
- Bedding and towels
- Appliances (e.g., refrigerator and microwave)
- Cleaning equipment
- Residential parking permits
- Electricity
- Gas
- Internet
- Water (if applicable)

Moving out can be expensive and it costs more than just the rent

Case Study:

The Real Cost of Moving

Now that Kelsey has finished college and has a good job, she's determined to move out on her own. She makes a budget, and after finding an apartment for $1,600 a month and allowing $100 a week for utilities, she feels comfortable that she can afford it on her take home salary of $3000 a month. What really surprises her is the cost of moving—over $2,300 before she even has her first night away from home. This includes her security deposit ($1,640), moving costs, and the purchase of a TV and microwave as well as a couple of items from a thrift store to supplement the furniture she's getting from her family. She decides to delay moving out for a couple of months till she has this money saved up.

Lesson: Living away from home costs more than just the monthly rent.

Preparing to Move Out

Finding a roommate

Be careful about your choice of roommate! There are not many things that are worse than living with someone you can't stand (unless you marry them as well), so this is definitely not the sort of decision to make at the end of a big night out. But think about it carefully and you can end up with someone who is a joy to live with.

A good roommate will be someone who:

- You have known for some time or at a minimum is a good friend of a good friend. Some people find success on the Internet, but you can't really be sure about what you're getting into till it's too late.

- Can be relied upon to contribute financially. Even if you are a model tenant, if they are late paying the rent, YOUR credit history may be affected. This might not matter now, but when you are trying to take out a loan to buy a house, you may get turned down.

- Will contribute to the running of the apartment – cleaning, getting the groceries, and general maintenance.

- Has the same hours as you – not a night shift worker when you like to have friends around for breakfast.

- Has the same habits as you – if you are a neat freak, and they like to live in a bomb site, it will only lead to unhappiness.

- Feels the same way as you about smoking, alcohol, and illegal drugs.

- Is similarly social – if you love to catch up at the end of the day and your roommate wants to be left alone, this can cause friction.

- Has similar feelings about ethical issues. For example, did you grow up on a cattle ranch and your roommate is a vegan? Do you feel strongly about the environment and your roommate thinks that all conservationists are crazy?

Laying Down the Ground Rules

Before you move in, you and your roommate(s) need to establish the ground rules. Some people like this all clearly written down and stuck on the refrigerator, while the idea of this freaks others out, but either way it's good to establish:

- What date you will all pay the rent. If you are paying separately, property managers prefer the rent to all be paid on the same day, not at a trickle.

- How you will manage the cleaning. Will you rotate tasks each week, or will you have dedicated jobs (e.g., you clean the bathroom; he'll do the vacuuming)?

- How you will manage food in the house. Will you pool together a specified sum each week for groceries? Or will you each have your own food?

Establish the ground rules before you move in

- How you will pay the bills. Again, will you pay from a pool? Or will you divide each bill as it arrives?

- How you feel about "special friends" sleeping over, and how often is okay. What about one-night stands? (This is important due to security issues.)

Finding Somewhere to Live

Contrary to finding a roommate, the best place to find somewhere to live IS on the Internet — there are lots of good websites around, and it will only take a short search to find one that might suit you. *Move.com* might be a good place to start, but there are lots more, so jump online and look. On all these websites you can register for free alerts about places that are likely to be a good fit; this will save you spending even more of your life on your computer! Be careful moving into an apartment belonging to a relative. You won't get a useful rental reference, and if things go wrong, it can sour the relationship.

If you can, use a parent as a co-signer. Property managers will always look at your rental history, and until you have one, they are going to see you as something of a risk. Having a parent as a co-signer will make them more likely to rent to you and will still mean that over time you gain a rental reference.

Checklist: A good place to live

Have you thought about these things? A good place to live will:

✔ Probably be on the second floor or above if it's an apartment, not on the first floor. First floor apartments may offer poorer security.

✔ Have a secure entrance and good street lighting. You should feel comfortable coming home alone at night.

✔ Have well-maintained and tidy communal areas such as the lobby, stairs, elevator, and laundry room. You can tell a lot about an apartment and the way it's run by what first greets you when you walk in the door.

✔ Have rooms oriented well. South-facing will give you sun through most of the day; east will give you morning sun; west will give you hot afternoon sun; and north may be dark.

✔ Have adequate parking. If there is no parking provided, is there adequate street parking or, even better, residents' parking on the street?

✔ Have suitable immediate surroundings. Perhaps there is a bar around the corner that will have late-night noise. Or a train station or freeway within hearing distance. Conversely, maybe there is a beautiful park across the road or a beach just a short stroll away.

✔ Have appropriate rooms in adequate condition. Can you live with the state of the carpets or that run-down kitchen and bathroom? Is that tiny little bedroom really going to be suitable?

✔ Have potential. Perhaps the apartment would be great with a coat of paint. Check first that it's okay with the property manager then go for it!

✔ Have adequate heating and cooling.

Once you have signed your rental agreement, if you find out that something is not to your taste, it is too late. You can't easily get out of it.

Lease Arrangements

Remember that rental agreements are legal contracts, so they should not be entered into lightly. Take home a copy of the agreement before you sign it, and don't be pressured into signing on the spot. These agreements are generally quite generic and are based on a standard set by a governing body, but you should read yours thoroughly, and if you can, ask your family to read it too. If there's something that is not clear to you, ask the property manager for clarification. You cannot change your mind once you have signed the agreement just because you misunderstood the meaning of a particular clause.

Whose names are on the agreement?

You need to decide whose name (or names) will be on the agreement. If you are sharing, it is most likely that you will have a "co-tenancy" arrangement — this means that everyone who is sharing will have their name on the agreement, and everyone will share responsibility for payment of the rent and the condition of the property. If one of the roommates moves out, they are still responsible for the property until their name is removed from the agreement, even if they are long gone. Be careful.

Subletting is where you just have one name on the agreement, and then that person allows others to become subtenants. It means you have control over who lives there and can get them to leave relatively easily if need be. But a big drawback is that it's ONLY YOU who is responsible to pay the rent or to keep the house in a reasonable condition, even if you are sharing with several others. You should check with the property manager whether you need to advise them if your roommates change.

Paying the security deposit

When you sign a rental contract, you will have to pay a sum of money that is held over until the end of your tenancy. This is called a security deposit. It covers:

- The cost of repairing any damage that has been caused to the house, whoever did it.

- Any cleaning that needs to be done once you leave.

- Replacement of any items that belong to the landlord.

- Unpaid rent.

- Bills that you should have paid but which are now left for the landlord to pay.

Depending on the level of the rent you are paying, the security deposit will generally be equal to one to two months' rent, so it can be substantial.

Security deposits are returned to you at the end of the lease if all is well. Remember that the security deposit will be returned to the people listed on the original security deposit form, so if you take over someone's place in a house, make sure that you contact your property manager to get the form changed to reflect this.

The security deposit can be substantial when you rent an apartment

Case Study:
Security Deposits Are Serious

Daniel moved into a house with two friends, Brittany and Andrew. The rent was $1,500 a month, and the security deposit was two months' rent, a total of $3,000, or $1,000 each.

During the three years that they lived there, Brittany moved out and Madison moved in. Time was tight on the day they all vacated, so they did a quick tidy up and jumped ship. Daniel was moving home before going overseas, and because he knew he'd be getting the security deposit money back, he spent the expected $1,000 on a new laptop. He put it on his credit card.

A few days later, he was horrified to find that the property manager wanted to keep $1,500 out of the security deposit—$200 for cleaning, $800 for replacing the carpet in a bedroom where some red wine had been spilled, and $500 for a new washing machine that they all thought had belonged to Brittany but which they actually saw on the Condition Report had belonged to the landlord. The amount they finally got back was $1,500 or $500 each. Daniel couldn't afford to pay off his credit card bill and was stuck with a $500 debt.

Lesson: Security deposits are serious.
Look after your rental property.

Condition report

When you go to collect the keys to your new place, the property manager will give you a completed Condition Report. You, as the tenant, should go through it very carefully once you get back to your rental property and fill out anything that has missed. Get on this quickly as it's like a bottle of milk — it goes bad quickly, and you don't want to have to get a new one.

Don't include maintenance items such as broken handles or blown light bulbs as these will be repaired during the time of your tenancy. (But do make sure you tell the property manager so they can be repaired.) This next point is important, so listen up! Take photos of any damage that has been omitted from the report, print off the photos in color, and then attach them to the report when you return it.

Advice on repairs

You need to establish with the property manager what the process is for scheduling repairs. Do they have a list of preferred suppliers that you can contact if there is an urgent problem? (If so, get a copy and stick it on your refrigerator.) Or is there a requirement that they themselves schedule all repairs? (Make sure you get the property manager's after-hours number as problems ALWAYS occur on weekends or at night.)

Do this before you move in so that when you have a problem with the apartment, you will be one step ahead.

Rent payment

While it can differ from contract to contract, it is likely that you will need to pay your rent once a month, in advance. Generally, you will pay electronically.

If you are sharing, choose one date every month that is rent-paying day. This makes it easier to work it out if there are any issues about whether payment has been made, and it will suit your property manager. Even if you are a model tenant, if anyone sharing the house is late in paying, your rental history will also be affected.

Keys

When you collect the keys, make sure you get a photocopy of the form confirming the number of keys and remotes you have taken. Most property managers will do this, and it will avoid problems at the end of the tenancy. Normally you will get one key per bedroom, but you can ask the property manager to make extra keys or you can do it yourself.

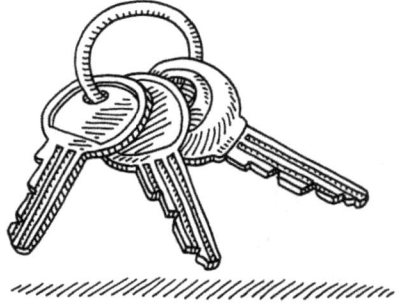

Another thing — don't lose a security key! It can be difficult to get extras made, so a replacement might cost you up to $50 per key.

Pets

While it can be harder to find a place that allows pets, it's not impossible. But make sure your roommates know beforehand, and never have a pet as a sneaky roommate. You do know that dogs can destroy gardens and puppies can destroy carpets, so how about a fish or hermit crab?

Preparing to Move In

Insurance

The landlord will insure for legal liability (e.g., if a guest breaks their leg falling down the stairs) and also for fire and flood damage to fixtures and fittings. This will cover flooring, lights, and ovens but will NOT cover your belongings. So if there's an overflowing sink or a leak from the apartment above that wrecks your computer, it's not their responsibility. Get your own renter's insurance!

Did you miss that? Get your own insurance! There are a number of companies that will insure the contents of your apartment/house for theft, fire, and flood or even just your belongings if you are sharing (just ask Mr. Google), and this can cost as little as $5 per week. Search *renter's insurance* and then apply online.

The landlord's insurance will not cover your belongings

You have two choices here: just insure your own belongings or insure the whole house/apartment's belongings (i.e., yours and your roommates'). I recommend that you just do your own — it can avoid grief later. It means you can insure for any amount you determine; you can decide how much of a deductible you want to pay (that's the part you pay before the insurance company kicks in), and you decide which items to include.

If you do decide to insure your roommate's belongings and yours together, remember that anyone who has their name on the policy can make changes to it. So your roommate can change the address of the policy (so you don't get any correspondence) and they can increase or decrease the value of the policy or the deductible payable.

What's included in my rental?

You'll need to think about what furniture and appliances you'll need when you move in. You should write a list for each room, detailing what you need and where you'll get it.

What I need to move out:

Kitchen

Fridge – the spare one from the garage
Microwave – Buy new
Table – Uncle Jimmy's old one
Oven – supplied

My Bedroom

Bed – the one from my bedroom
Nightstand – from the thrift store
Cupboard – ? maybe from mom
Mirror – ?

Second Bedroom

Desk & chair – from my bedroom
Bookshelf – thrift store
Rug – the old one from the garage

Living Room

Sofa and armchair – from the spare room
Coffee table – thrift store
TV – buy one new
TV stand – thrift store

You will need to check your contract, but generally the following items will be included:

- All fixtures and fittings, such as blinds, flooring, and light fixtures with working light bulbs (although you will need to replace them once they blow)
- Smoke detectors
- The oven, stovetop, refrigerator, and dishwasher

Connecting utilities

When you rent a property, you will find that it comes without any electricity, gas, phone, Internet, or water. Connecting the first four (electricity, gas, phone, and Internet) will be your responsibility, while connecting and paying for water may be either the landlord's responsibility (if you are in a block of apartments and there is only one water meter) or your responsibility (if it is a house or an apartment that has its own water meter).

There are two ways to connect your utilities. You can do an Internet search to work out which service providers will give you the best value. A comparison website can help. Then you can call them individually to get the connection process started.

Alternatively, an easy way out is to get a connection company to take care of it for you. You can still specify which provider you would prefer (although getting the best deal might be trickier), but there is no charge to you, and it is extremely easy. There are several companies out there (enter *connection utilities* into your Internet search engine).

A couple of things to remember:

- Think about whether you want a home phone line. Apart from your parents, the only people who'll use it are slimy people wanting to "fix" the terrible virus on your computer and charities seeking donations. It's old technology, and you won't use it much — consider not having one.

- Don't sign up for a phone or Internet plan that is longer than your rental agreement (e.g., don't sign up for a 24-month Internet plan when your rental agreement is only for 12 months).

- Make sure the names on the utilities match the names on the lease agreement (i.e., don't put your name alone on the electricity bill, as then you have a legal responsibility to pay it, not your roommates).

What time can I move in?

Make sure that you confirm with the property manager what time you want to move into your rental property. Many apartment blocks have specified times to move in or out, particularly on weekends. This is in order not to disturb the other tenants.

When Something Goes Wrong

Problems with the property

During the time that you are renting a property, it's pretty likely that you will have some sort of problem. Generally, <u>urgent repairs</u> include the following:

- A toilet that doesn't work or is blocked
- A leak in your roof or flooding of the apartment
- A gas leak or electricity fault
- No water, electricity, or gas to the apartment
- A hot water service or heater that doesn't work
- Anything that makes the apartment unsafe, unhygienic, or inaccessible

If the problem is during working hours, you should contact the property manager immediately by both email and phone (phone because it's quick; email because you will have a written record of the problem and when you contacted them).

For after-hours repairs, hopefully you will have worked out what the preferred process is before you moved in. This could be contacting the appropriate repairer from the list that you put on your refrigerator when you first moved in or contacting an emergency number provided. Either way, make sure you send an email as well so that it's on record.

For <u>non-urgent repairs</u>, you should also advise the agent in writing, and these should then be done within a reasonable timeframe.

Problems with your roommate

Even if you followed the advice above in *Finding a Roommate* and *Laying Down the Ground Rules* above, things can still go wrong. First of all, don't worry! It will all work out.

If you are unhappy living with someone, it's most likely that they are having issues with you too. It sounds easier than it is, but try to have a low-key talk. Explain the problem you are having with them, and see if you can come to a solution. As always, it's better to broach small issues as they arise rather than sitting on them until they become huge problems.

If it's clear that you can't work out your difficulties, tell your roommate that you will move out as soon as you find someone to take over your part of the rental agreement. Once you find someone, both you and the new tenant will need to advise the agent and attend to any required paperwork.

If you can't find anyone to take over, unfortunately you will have to grit your teeth and bide your time until the end of the lease. Tell your roommate that you will be giving notice to the property manager that you will be leaving when the lease finishes, and that if they wish to continue staying in the house, they will need to find someone to take over your position on the lease.

Remember that if you are sharing an apartment, you are both responsible for any payments due and for the condition of the house, so try to work out any issues of this nature early on. Whatever happens in the house will reflect on your tenancy report.

Eviction

Rest assured that this doesn't usually happen! But this time it has. Oh dear.

Non-payment of rent

Eviction is most usually for non-payment of rent but can also be for maliciously causing damage or putting other people in danger as well as using the premises for illegal purposes. You will be given notice in writing about when you are required to vacate. If you do not do so by the specified time, the matter will go to the governing body. Clearly you should avoid this.

Eviction is usually for non-payment of rent or malicious damage

Noise

With regards to noise, remember that not everyone wants to party until 3 a.m., so if you are being too noisy, you will be given written notice about the problem, and if you continue to turn the volume up, then the matter will revert to the relevant governing body as above. Be careful — this will affect your tenancy report, and you will miss out on a good reference for future rentals.

Unclean rental property

While you are living in your rental property, you will have to endure inspections. The property manager will have a good look around (though just at the surface — they're not going to go all weird and go through your cupboards) and then they will complete a report. Remember that there are rules limiting the number of times they can come through per year and how much notice you need to be given, so if you think it's too often, it can be wise to check the regulations in your state. You can get evicted if your place is very unclean, so make an effort!

End of Tenancy

So you've come to the end of your tenancy, and you are all going your separate ways. Don't forget to hand in your notice. (The property manager will have advised you of the period required, usually between 14–28 days.) And remember that you were paying your rent in advance? That means there is no payment due when you move out. Yay!

If there has been any damage, it can be quite easy to fix. For instance, you can replace a hinge on a cupboard or spot clean a stain on the carpet yourself. Once you've done what you can, make sure the place is really clean, take photos, and then return the key to the office. Don't assume the property manager has a key, and don't be late — if you are, you will continue to be charged rent day by day. The property manager will do an inspection that you should attend if you can and then will do one of two things:

1. Return the security deposit. (Well done, you excellent tenants!)

2. Draw your attention to damage and the required repairs that will be funded out of your initial security deposit. It is of course within your power to formally object, but this can be a lengthy process subject to your state's laws and is to be avoided if at all possible.

Once the security deposit (or part of it) is returned, leave a forwarding address with the property manager, and say adios to your roommates. Happy days.

Five Top Tips

1. If you don't have a rental history, see if your parents will act as co-signers. Happy property manager, happy you!

2. Put a list of the manager's preferred repairers as well as your utility suppliers on the refrigerator. Don't lose it, as that'll be the day the power goes out.

3. Don't sign up for a home phone or Internet plan that is longer than your lease (e.g., a 24-month Internet plan on a 12-month lease).

4. Use a connection company to connect your natural gas, electricity, and water.

5. Keep your place clean. Yep, you can get evicted if it's too dirty.

CHAPTER 3

Finding That Perfect Job

S o you've moved out and things are looking a little grim on the money front. You're not much of a card shark, and you're too clumsy to be a cat burglar. Looks like you'll have to get a job. Darn.

Haven't Got Time to Read the Whole Chapter? Read This.

1. Use your networks. If you haven't worked before, you might think you don't have any, but think of your school friends, parents' friends, sports friends, people at the gym or the park, and your neighbors. Get out there and talk to everyone — often people like to help.

2. You need a good résumé as a starting point when you are looking for a job. There's not just one perfect format, so get advice, go online, and spend some time developing a good one.

3. Become familiar with and practice the STAR (Situation, Task, Action, Result) technique for answering questions in competency-based interviews. This gives you a framework to answer questions when the interviewers ask you to describe a situation where you displayed one of the skills they're looking for.

4. Prepare yourself for your interview. Think of questions you're likely to be asked, and work out your answers in advance, do some research, get in some practice, and be as friendly and relaxed as you can be.

5. Be careful how your online presence portrays you as a potential employee. When the interviewer asks you to show them your Facebook page, are you going to be happy with what they see? More importantly, are they?

What Type of Job Are You After?

If this is your first time in the workforce, you might be looking for something part-time that will fit in with your college schedule. This could involve babysitting, flipping burgers, or just vacation work between semesters. Keep an eye out for jobs advertised on noticeboards, and then you will need to start pounding the pavement, dropping in on likely businesses with your résumé in hand. A smile on your face will go a long way. It can be really hard without experience, but everyone was in the same boat once, and you'll get there. Keep at it.

Alternatively, you may now be looking for that first full-time job. This is really daunting territory as there's so much more at stake. You could be in this job for several years, and while changing jobs often can be a fact of life with part-time work, it's not so acceptable for permanent jobs. This chapter will help you in your search.

Where to Look

Use networks

Everyone has networks that can be useful in looking for a job. Perhaps you play tennis with someone who is working in an interesting company, or your mom's best friend has a job you think you'd really enjoy. Is there a teacher from your old school or a professor at college that you really clicked with and who might be able to help? Maybe your friend's employer is looking for an extra hand, or how about the people you've met when you've done work experience or volunteering? Make sure that you talk to everyone about what it is you're looking for, and ask for their assistance if you think they might be able to help. Don't be worried that you are taking advantage of people — they are usually happy to help.

Your aim in using your networks is to get a foot in the door and to differentiate yourself from everyone else who is applying for the same job. Perhaps you'll get the chance to meet with someone from Human

Resources or get the name of a person you can talk with. After that, it will be up to you, but often the first step is the hardest.

Research

One way to get a job is to directly approach companies you are interested in. Start by doing some research in your industry. Who would you like to work for?

Directly approach companies you would like to work for

Draw up a potential list of target companies, find out some more about them, and then give them a call (see *How to Cold Call a Company* coming up in this chapter).

Where do you find a job?

Twenty years ago every advertised job was listed in the local newspapers. It was a simple matter to get the Saturday papers and a big red marker and to circle the ones that looked appealing. These days, you'll find that while newspapers have days dedicated to certain industries, the bulk of jobs aren't in the newspaper at all. You might be lucky and find one, but you'd do better to look online.

Your first stop should be to get onto a business networking website such as *LinkedIn*[19]. Here you can upload your résumé, look for jobs that might be of interest, research industries and companies, join discussion groups, and further build your network. Even more importantly, though, is the fact that employers can find you.

You should also look at job websites. There are many out there, but some with the highest traffic include *Indeed, Monster,* and *CareerBuilder*. While each site is slightly different, you can generally search for available jobs using key words, salary levels, location, and industry. You can also set up alerts so you are automatically notified when a suitable job is listed, and when you find one, you can apply via the website.

Volunteering and internships

Sometimes you have the opportunity to volunteer or do an internship at a company you might be interested in. This gives you a chance to get to know the organization better and to get some experience, but it also gives them a risk-free way of getting to see you in action. Play your cards right and have luck on your side, and they may end up taking you on permanently...and paying you!

How to Cold Call a Company

Cold calling a company is enough to put fear into anyone's heart. It's awful, but here's a way to do it with the least angst possible:

- Identify the company you want to approach.
- Call and ask to speak to the HR (Human Resources) department. If possible, listen hard and try to get the name of the person you are being transferred to, either when reception says their name or when the person answers the phone. Write it down.
- Introduce yourself by name, and say that you are interested in finding employment.
- Say what sort of job you're after, what your skills and experience are, and why you like their company. Be brief — people are busy.
- Ask if you can please send in a résumé.
- Thank them for their time.
- Now that you've had the phone conversation, follow up with a letter addressed to the person you spoke with starting with "Further to our conversation today...." That will get your letter to the top of the pile. And don't forget to attach your résumé!

There, was that so bad?

How to Create a Written Application

A written application for a job consists of a cover letter and an accompanying résumé. (Sometimes "curriculum vitae," or CV, can be used interchangeably with the word "résumé" but they are basically the same thing.)

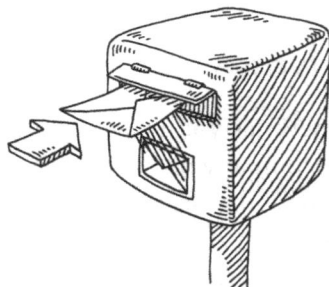

You should put together a master résumé that includes all your skills, experience, and qualifications then tailor it for each job application. This is in no way suggesting that you tell a few fibs (you're not that sort of person, are you?) but just that you include experience and information that is relevant or appropriate for the job at hand. Never, ever lie on a résumé about your skills or experience or be boastful or unrealistic about what you can achieve for the company. It is worth noting here that there are enormous amounts of websites devoted to writing résumés, and many will have samples of résumés and accompanying letters, so look till you find a style that suits you. Don't plagiarize (no! no! no!), but make use of the ideas you find. Alternatively, look below.

General formatting and layout

- Use a spell checker and a grammar checker as any typos or spelling mistakes are deadly. Then get a literate friend to check over your résumé for you.

- Did you miss that? Make sure that you get someone else to read your résumé and correct any mistakes you might have made. We all make them, but nothing will turn off a potential employer faster than a stupid mistake — it makes you look sloppy or, even worse, not particularly smart.

- Use plain professional English with no abbreviations unless they are so common that anyone reading them will understand them.

- Use standard white copying paper. You should use a simple font such as Times New Roman, 12 point. Now is not the time to use colored paper or the Zapf Dingbats font to express your inner quirkiness — it will just make you stand out (but in a really bad way).

Use a spell checker and a grammar checker

- Include a footer with your name and email address on every page in case the pages get separated.

- Leave large margins and lots of white space. It looks much more controlled and aesthetically pleasing. If there is little white space, it can look like you've rushed your résumé or that you are so desperate to impress that you are including everything.

- Use bold for headings, and bullet points throughout for clarity

Leave large margins and lots of white space

- If sending your résumé by email, send it as a .pdf to make sure that the formatting doesn't get messed up.

Cover letter

- This should be written on one side of the page on white copy paper.

- Write a new letter for each job application — it can be easy to spot a "one size fits all" letter.

- Address the letter to a specific person, and keep it formal (e.g., address it to "Mr. Jones", not to "Andrew" or "to whom it may concern").

- Say why you are interested in the job and the industry.

- Make sure your letter explains why you think you would be suitable for the position and what you can bring to the organization.

- Make sure you pick up a few key words from the advertisement and include them (but try not to be too obvious!).

Résumé

- Don't make it too long — two or three pages is fine and only one page if it's for a part-time job.

- Leave out anything from your master résumé that is not relevant to the job for which you are applying.

- Make sure that points you wish to highlight are easy to see and, if there is more than one page, that they fall on the first page. This will make them more evident to the interviewer, who may well be sifting through piles and piles of applications and wishing they were on a desert island somewhere.

- Remember, the heading should be your name and not "Résumé."

Sample Layout for Your Résumé

There are hundreds of ways to present your résumé, and yours will be slightly different from your friend's, which in turn won't be the same as your dad's. Don't stress — go online and do some research, or use the following as a guide. Concentrate on making it professional, clear, and factual. The aim is to make you seem so appealing that they will want to take your application one step further.

Contact details

- First name and last name as heading (don't worry about your middle name)
- Address
- Email address
- Cell phone number
- Some people like to include their date of birth, gender (if your name doesn't give it away), or marital status, but there are a number of reasons why this is becoming less common — for instance because it has nothing to do with how good you will be at your job.

Key skills

- Write a list of your key skills, including personal and business skills, computer skills, and languages. Make sure you include those that are mentioned in the advertisement if you have them.

Include a list of your key skills in your résumé

College education

- Work in reverse order, so last comes first.
- List the date of completion, the name of the course or degree, and the institution you attended.
- Include any relevant details that relate to the position, including scholarships and awards.

High school education

- This section should be shorter than the section on college education.
- List the details of your final year at school, your high school grade point, and your SAT or ACT score.
- Also list any major achievements, awards, or leadership positions and any overseas study.

Employment history

- Again, in reverse date order, list your employment history, including your starting and ending dates, the job title, the name of the organization, and bullet points of your key responsibilities.
- Don't automatically disregard any part-time jobs you have held — there may be skills that you have developed that are transferable. This is particularly true of large organizations that are known for the quality of their training, such as McDonald's.

Professional memberships

- List the period of your membership, the organization's name, and the level of membership.

Professional training & further development

- In reverse-date order, list the name of any training courses you have completed, the length of the course, and the provider.

Volunteer work

- List any volunteer work you have completed, including the name of the organization, dates you worked there, and your role. List bullet points of key responsibilities if these are not self-evident.
- You could include work with religious groups, sporting organizations, organizations for the elderly, etc.

Extra-curricular activities and hobbies

- List your hobbies and extra-curricular activities. Don't include too much detail, but try to think about what might be relevant or appropriate for the job at hand.

References

- Make sure that your references agree to support you in the job application, and ask them if they mind being included BEFORE you mention them in your résumé. Never include someone's name if you haven't yet asked, even if you are 100% sure that they will support you. It's also a good idea to ask if you can use their name in multiple applications rather than approaching them before every job application.
- List the name, title, and contact details of your references, but at this stage do not include anything they may have written about you, unless requested to do so.

- Don't go overboard, make them relevant, and do what the employer asks; if they want two references, give them two, not seven.
- And don't forget to thank your references, particularly if you get the job.

Make sure that your references agree to support you beforehand

Advice About Interviews

So you've got an interview! Well done! Whether the interview will be at a distance (say by phone or electronic communication) or in person, you need to make some preparations beforehand.

Prepare yourself

Go on to the organization's website, and do some research about the company and, if you can, your particular division or area of work. Think about what's required in the job and what skills or competencies you might need to do the job well. These are often listed in the advertisement.

This preparation can be extremely useful when you come across a competency-based interview. This means that instead of a free-flowing talk, the interviewers will be using the time to establish whether or not you have the required skills for the job. You may be asked about a situation that has arisen in the past and how you handled it. So before you have the interview, you need to put together examples of how you have previously demonstrated the required competencies, and a very good way of doing this is to use the STAR technique: Situation, Task, Action, and Result.

In summary, look at what competencies will be required in the position, and ahead of time, think of examples from your previous work life (or personal life if this is your first job), which can be answered using the STAR technique. Don't make it obvious to the interviewer that you are answering using this method – the aim is to make them think that you are just providing a coherent answer to the question. Be brief to keep the interviewer's interest, and be specific, using names, so that it is more realistic. And don't fib!

Case Study:
Using the STAR Technique

Ashley was being interviewed for a job as a program leader at the local college. She had thought hard about examples from her previous work life and how they related to the competencies required, so when the interviewer asked her to talk about a time when she had to problem solve under pressure, Ashley was able to answer fluently.

"I was working as a program leader in the diploma of economics course, and late in the afternoon, I got a call saying that Joshua, the lecturer for the macroeconomics class that evening, was unwell and couldn't attend (Situation).

"I had to quickly find a replacement so that the students hadn't all traveled downtown after work only to find that the lecturer was absent (Task).

"I consulted the list of macroeconomics lecturers to find a replacement and discovered that Lauren was not scheduled to work that night, so I contacted her to see if she was available. She was. I then organized for Joshua to email his lecture plan and notes to her (Action).

"When the students arrived, Lauren explained the situation and proceeded with the class as normal (Result).

Lesson: Prepare to use the STAR technique to answer competency-based questions.

In addition to thinking about the STAR technique, think of other questions you might be asked, and practice answers to them. For example, they might ask you how your skills might make you suitable for the job or how your previous experience might be relevant. Don't forget the old favorites "What are your strengths and weaknesses?" and "Where do you see yourself in five years' time?"

Practice answers to key questions you think you might be asked

And finally, think of some questions that you can ask. These could be about career paths or company structure, or you could throw in one that will indicate you've done your homework (e.g., "How do you see the recent changes in your parent company affecting the local organization?") Don't ask about money. Be prepared to discuss it if they raise it; otherwise, save it for a later stage of the recruitment process.

Practice makes perfect

If you are at college, take advantage of the careers office as some offer one-on-one interview practice; otherwise, practice with a supportive friend. If all else fails, try the dog. (I personally find that dogs are quite non-judgmental.)

Some people swear by standing in front of the mirror and practicing, although I usually feel like an idiot and end up being distracted. (Why's my hair standing up like that? What's that strange shadow on my face?) But give it a try — if it works for you, that's great.

And during the interview

Be prepared to sell yourself. This is one time when it won't work in your best interest to be modest, but never lie about what you have done or will be able to do for the company. Try to frame your weaknesses in a positive light (e.g., "One weakness I have is that I tend to be a perfectionist."), but don't be too obvious.

Don't speak too quickly, and don't mumble. If they ask you to repeat yourself, it doesn't necessarily mean they are reacting to something you've said in a negative way — maybe it's just that their years of hanging out in nightclubs means their hearing's shot.

And finally, try to keep your nerves under control. It might be important, but it's not the only company in the world and certainly not the only job. What's the worst that can happen? Maybe you'll vomit on the interview desk or drop the "F" bomb five times by mistake. So what? It's unlikely to change the course of your life and will make a great story later on.

Interviews at a Distance

If you have sent in your résumé, you may be asked for a phone or video conference interview.

Phone interviews are tricky as there are no non-verbal cues

Checklist: Phone or video conference interview

✔ Go to the bathroom beforehand and have a drink of water handy but no food! It'll just sound weird if you are crunching throughout the phone call.

✔ Have some tissues available in case. No, not because you'll be crying! You might need to (surreptitiously) blow your nose.

✔ Do you need any papers? Are there documents that might be useful? Have them on hand.

✔ Have a pen and paper to write down questions or make notes.

✔ Make sure that you have turned off your cell phone (unless they are calling you on it – duh), tell your roommates to keep quiet, put the dog outside, and shut yourself in a quiet room.

✔ Make yourself feel professional – don't do the interview in your underwear! And even more so if it's a video interview…

✔ Sound interested and friendly. Phone interviews are tricky as there are no non-verbal cues, so this is even more important than normal. Try to remember the name of the interviewer, and don't get distracted – hey, what was that out the window?

✔ At the end of the interview, thank them then the following day make sure you send a thank you email, re-expressing your interest in the job and saying that you are looking forward to hearing from them.

Interviews in Person

Or maybe you've got an interview in person.

Checklist: Personal interview

✔ Before the big day, call and ask about the format of the interview and if there is anything else that you can send in that would be useful to the interviewers. This shows you are interested and have initiative.

✔ Don't be late! Plan ahead and aim to be early even if you're absolutely sure how long it will take to get there.

✔ Dress appropriately, and of course make sure your clothes are clean and well-ironed. Make sure your shoes are in a good state of health too.

✔ Once you arrive and have checked in, turn off your phone. Yep, off.

✔ Be friendly and confident, even if you don't feel it. And, of course, be polite.

✔ At the end, ask what the process is from here on in, and thank them for their time.

✔ Again, shoot them off a thank you email re-expressing your interest in the job and that you are looking forward to hearing from them.

✔ You can follow up with a phone call if you don't hear from them in the next week or so. If they have said not to call, then (yep, you're right) don't.

And one final thought

It is not unheard of for employers to check what you've been doing online, and they will make judgments about you based on what they find. So think about how you want to be perceived, and if necessary, delete those postings that might form the wrong impression.

(And by the way, if you have zero online presence, you will be well sought after for a job as a spy.)

Good luck!

Five Top Tips

1. Make sure your résumé is perfect in terms of grammar, spelling, and typos. Get your smartest friend to check it out or even your parents.

2. Write a new cover letter for each application. It's easy to spot one that is generic, and it's insulting to the interviewer to think you can't be bothered with writing a new one.

3. Be prepared to sell yourself in an interview. It might feel weird telling strangers how wonderful you are, but now is not the time to be self-effacing.

4. But that doesn't mean lying or exaggerating. We want the truth, the whole truth, and nothing but the truth — but it can be sugar-coated. And in fact the whole truth might be too revealing ….

5. And a no-brainer — don't be late for your interview! Plan to arrive half an hour early, and spend the time quietly practicing and calming yourself.

CHAPTER 4

Kitchen Essentials

W e've all got some Jamie Oliver in us, but maybe this is the first time you have had your own kitchen and tried to manage your own food budget. Do you feel excited? Or maybe terrified? Don't worry — I'm here to help.

Haven't Got Time to Read the Whole Chapter? Read This.

1. Raw meat can contain lots of bacteria, so keep it away from cooked foods. Make sure you wash the plate that your uncooked steak was on before you put the cooked version back. Clean up meaty spills on your countertop, and store raw meat on the bottom shelf of your refrigerator to avoid it dripping on other food.

2. If both your larder and your wallet are empty, go visit a "pay as much as you can" restaurant. Or look to see where you can volunteer and then be fed. Think churches, missions, and soup kitchens.

3. Make food gifts for your friends and family. A homemade cake on a birthday can be more meaningful than an expensive gift, and jams and chutneys last nearly forever and are always welcome.

4. Cook at home.

5. Did you miss that? Cook at home. Avoid restaurants - they can be expensive and bad for you. Make them a big treat for special occasions and not a weekly occurrence.

Basic Kitchen Equipment

You may have come from a kitchen that has been really well equipped, and if you've cooked before, you're used to having whatever you need at hand. It's unrealistic to expect that your own kitchen will be that well-stocked at the start, but here's a list of essentials you can work towards owning.

You can get most of these items secondhand at the local thrift store, but you'll find that over time friends and family will come up with things they don't need and which they don't mind giving you. You certainly don't need to rush out and buy everything listed here on the first day out of home.

Checklist: Kitchen equipment

✔ A couple of non-stick saucepans, say one large and one small, and with glass lids if you can. Glass lids make all the difference as you can check what's going on in there without opening the lid and losing all that heat. They absolutely must be non-stick — life's too short to be scrubbing saucepans! If you are concerned about the safety of non-stick saucepans, never fear and check out the *Low Fat Cooking* website.[2]

✔ At least one non-stick fry pan. If it has reasonable sides and can double as a wok, so much the better.

✔ Something to stir with. I would suggest two wooden spoons of different sizes.

✔ A cutting board. Wood is best to keep your knives sharp. If you have space for two, also get a plastic one that can tolerate the dishwasher and use it for chicken and meat. The dishwasher will kill any residual bugs that might make you ill.

- ✔ Something to scrape with. A silicone spatula is good.
- ✔ A large mixing bowl. This can double as a salad bowl. If you need a small one, use a dessert bowl.
- ✔ A colander (also known as a strainer or "that thing with holes in it").
- ✔ A slotted spoon (a big spoon with holes for draining, say, peas out of the saucepan — also known as "that other thing with holes in it").
- ✔ A pair of tongs. Cheap ones are perfect.
- ✔ A slotted turner, say, for turning over your piece of fish or sliding cookies off the tray.
- ✔ A baking tray to fit your oven. New ovens come with their own, but at a rental property, they have often gone home with previous tenants.
- ✔ An 8" round cake pan. Silicone ones are very easy to use but are unsteady, so if you have one of these, sit it on your baking tray to cook. An aluminum one is fine too but can be a nuisance as you'll need to line it with parchment paper each time you use it.
- ✔ A 12-hole muffin pan. Again, silicone is great, but sit it on a tray to cook.
- ✔ A pie plate — good for savory or dessert pies or puddings.
- ✔ A small hand mixer. It will make life a lot easier, although a wooden spoon and lots of effort can give the same result. Keep your eyes open and you'll be able to pick one up for next to nothing.
- ✔ If you're into soups, a blender — hand (stick) or otherwise.
- ✔ A cooling rack
- ✔ A sifter or a fine sieve
- ✔ A veggie peeler
- ✔ A grater

✔ A garlic crusher

✔ A round cookie cutter

✔ Individual measuring cups (1 cup, ½ cup, ¼ cup, ⅓ cup) or a large measuring cup with these measurements marked on it.

✔ Measuring spoons (1 tablespoon, 1 teaspoon, ½ teaspoon, ¼ teaspoon)

✔ Parchment paper, aluminum foil, plastic food wrap (Saran wrap)

✔ A pastry brush (okay, maybe not essential, but you'll be surprised how often you use it)

✔ A whisk (fun to have, especially if you make sauces or custard)

✔ Something to test whether a cake is cooked — a metal skewer, toothpicks, a purpose-designed cake tester or a bamboo skewer. If you choose the latter, buy a pack, keep one for cake testing and use the rest for making chicken-on-a-stick.

✔ This book of course and something to access the Internet so you can look up recipes. There are a million recipe websites, and you'll soon learn which ones suit your budget and your palate. If you can't find what you're looking for, it doesn't exist. Yet.

Food Budgeting

You're going to realize pretty quickly once you move out of home that one, the refrigerator doesn't refill itself (darn!), and two, food is really expensive. You'll need to stick to a budget or else getting the groceries will eat up all your available cash. Try these tips to get more bang for your buck:

1. Write a list, and don't shop when you're hungry — the theory is that if you do, you'll buy more.

2. Check your refrigerator before you write your shopping list, and try to plan meals so that you use up everything you have. Be creative,

Write a grocery list and stick to it

and don't let food go bad. There are websites that can help you. One that is fun to use is *Big Oven*[3] — just enter three ingredients you have in your refrigerator and it will give you recipes. Sweet.

Set a budget for your weekly grocery shop and don't spend more

3. Don't be afraid of doing your fruit and veggie shopping at a big supermarket. People will tell you to shop at the local store, and I can see why — it's good to support local businesses, and there's a feeling that the products are less processed and have lower food miles. All good reasons. But remember that supermarkets have such massive turnover you're pretty sure of getting fresh produce there, and if you find you have a problem with something, you can always take it back for a refund, no questions asked.

4. Allocate a certain amount of money for your weekly shop and stick to it. Or if this doesn't work so well for you, only take the amount of cash with you that you have allocated for groceries, and leave your ATM card at home.

5. Okay – this is going to appear obvious, but buy food when it's on sale and when it's in season. For example, don't buy your strawberries in winter; they're either hot-housed or have come from a looooooooong way away, and that makes them more expensive and less fresh (which probably equals less tasty).

6. Look at buying generic brands. You'll need to work out over time which ones are okay, but you will be pretty safe with all your basic ingredients such as flour, sugar, milk, etc.

7. Buy non-perishables such as toilet paper, laundry detergent, and canned tomatoes in bulk if you can afford to and have the storage space.

8. Get to know the prices of things you often buy so you can tell where they are the cheapest.

9. If there's one nearby, make use of discount food stores – they have cheap food because it is near its use-by date or the packaging has been damaged.

10. Eat at home. Eat at home. Repeat after me. Eat at home. Eating out at restaurants can be expensive, and is often unhealthy. Okay, it's great for a treat, but you can cook up a feast at home quicker than you can pick up a meal – how about an omelet, some Spaghetti Carbonara, or a big bowl of soup? Less than 20 minutes and you're done.

11. Limit alcohol. Yep, lots of reasons to do it, and one of them is cost.

12. Go vegetarian, or at least try it a couple of times a week. You'll be helping the environment and also saving money. In terms of dollar cost of protein, meat's right up there. Try eggs or lentils. And speaking of lentils, even if you're having a meat meal, if it happens to be made of ground beef, throw in a handful. They're healthy, bulk the meal out, and are cheap.

13. Your freezer is your friend – did you know you can freeze bread and cakes perfectly? Just make sure they are well sealed in a freezer bag or they can get that white burnt texture of freezer burn. Don't use Saran wrap or a bread bags as these are permeable and your food won't stay fresh. In the case of bread, you don't even need to defrost it before

you cook it; just pop it in the toaster. You can also freeze cream, milk, butter, and citrus fruit for use in cooking at a later date.

14. Meats are also good to freeze. Buy on special and freeze, particularly cheaper cuts, which survive the cold environment wonderfully. But don't keep frozen meat longer than 6–12 months (and ground beef for only three months).

Make food gifts to give to your friends

15. Don't buy water in bottles. It's a total waste of money, and all those bottles have to end up somewhere. Here's a horrible statistic — 60 million bottles A DAY (yep, you read that right) are thrown away in the U.S., and the water in those bottles costs up to 4,000 times more than tap water.[4]

16. Make food gifts to give to people. How about a homemade birthday cake? A quiche or a pot of soup? It is certainly more meaningful than anything you could pick up at a store.

17. Have a green thumb? Try to grow veggies in whatever space you have available. You can start small with herbs or tomatoes that are easy to grow in a pot and then move on to other veggies. Speak to your neighbors to find out what works for them as they have the same micro-climate as you.

Essential Food Items to Keep On Hand

Sometimes you just don't have the money or the time to go to the store, so it's good to know you can make a meal out of what's already in your cupboard. Here is a list of food items you should always have on hand and which will allow you to cook a decent meal. It looks long, but these are all cheap and, apart from the eggs and butter, will stay fresh in your pantry. You should stock up on them when you see them on sale. Unlike the kitchen equipment, if you can afford them, I'd buy them all on day one of living away from home.

From the list below, you can make fried rice, tuna pasta, omelets, veggie curry, porridge, eggs on toast, butter cake, tuna stir-fry, pasta with corn sauce, plain cookies, French toast, risotto, sandwiches…the list goes on…

Checklist: Basics to have on hand

✔ All-purpose flour
✔ Sugar
✔ Eggs
✔ Butter
✔ Baking powder
✔ Oil
✔ Rice
✔ Oats
✔ Pasta
✔ Bread (store in the freezer)
✔ Frozen peas
✔ Canned tuna
✔ Canned tomatoes
✔ Canned corn
✔ Curry powder or paste (red Thai curry paste is a good first choice)
✔ Soy sauce
✔ Bouillon cubes (start with vegetable; then expand to meat and chicken)
✔ Milk

Food Storage

Cupboards

If you can, store all open packs of dry goods in containers in your pantry or cupboards to avoid moths. Moths are pesky critters lying dormant in packs of food and ready to spring to life at the first chance so they can contaminate other food in your pantry. You know you have a moth problem if you see your food clumping together weirdly with wispy bits of what looks like spider web clinging to the edges of the container. I'm pretty sure moths don't have teeth, but you wouldn't believe it as they can eat through plastic bags. Ugh. Common wisdom says that bay leaves can deter moths, but I've never found this advice to be very helpful.

There's nothing much worse than moths in your pantry, apart from rats and mice. To keep rodents at bay, clean up any spills or drips immediately, and make sure you wipe off the shelves in your pantry every now and then. Borrowing a cat is a good non-toxic (at least for you) way of keeping rats and mice away.

Putting food in containers and wiping countertops will also help keep ants away. If you do end up with an ant problem, there are ant-killing liquids you dot around the place that are very effective. Personally, I'd rather rely on keeping things clean or even just put up with the ants than have these chemicals near food, but lots of people swear by them.

Store wine in a dry area with an even temperature, and don't move it around too much. Yep, a cellar is perfect, but so is a cupboard. If the wine has real corks, store it on its side.

Fridge

Notice that the first place you visit when you go back to your parents' place is the refrigerator? That's because everyone knows the refrigerator can be the source of all joy!

You need to remember a few things to keep you and your food healthy. Store meat on the lowest shelf in the refrigerator so any drips can't fall onto food stored on a shelf below. This is to avoid cross-contamination of other foods with bacteria from the raw meat. Similarly, don't ever put cooked meat back on a plate that has held raw meat — wash it in between.

Store meat on the lowest shelf in the refrigerator

Remember that meat (particularly chicken) and seafood, eggs, and dairy products pose the greatest risk in terms of food poisoning. You need to store these in the refrigerator and not leave them sitting out on the countertop. So that means you shouldn't defrost food in the sink — plan ahead and do it on a plate in the refrigerator or in the microwave on the defrost setting.

Case Study:

Ryan Gets Food Poisoning

Before Ryan left for work, he pulled out a great-looking steak from the freezer and put it in the kitchen sink to thaw. That night he came home late from work, so he quickly put the steak on the grill, and leaving the plate next to the grill, went to the fridge and put together a salad. He finished cooking the steak, put it on the plate, and helped himself to the salad. It was an excellent meal.

That night he was violently ill and threw up most of the night. That's when he remembered the advice about not defrosting food in the sink and not using dirty plates for cooked food.

Lesson: Defrost meat in the fridge, and never use a plate that has held raw meat for cooked food.

If you can, store foods in the refrigerator in glass or ceramic containers. You can use plastic wrap over the top, but try to avoid it touching the food. There is some concern about chemicals leaching from plastic into food, particularly if the food is hot, acidic, fatty, or salty.[5]

And don't forget to wipe out your refrigerator every now and then with hot soapy water. You can add some vanilla to the water to make your refrigerator smell sweet. If something spills, wipe it up quickly — it's amazing how difficult things can be to get off the walls or shelves of the refrigerator once they're dried on.

Leftovers

When you don't have lots of cash to spend, make sure you use up any leftovers in your refrigerator. Apart from making sense economically, it can stretch your boundaries in terms of creativity. Look at the *Big Oven* website for ideas on using odd blends of ingredients.[6]

Checklist: What to do with leftovers

- ✔ Stale bread can be chopped up into cubes, sprayed with oil, and cooked in the oven to make croutons for soup.
- ✔ Bread can also be dipped in beaten egg and vanilla and fried in butter to make delicious French toast.
- ✔ Make over-ripe bananas into banana bread (see recipe to follow).
- ✔ Throw the hard rind of Parmesan cheese into a stew or soup — it will give a great flavor to the soup.
- ✔ Leftover meat makes a great curry — cut it all up, fry with some curry paste, and add coconut milk to make a feast fit for a king. Or heat it up in the microwave in some gravy.

✔ Cakes or cookies can be crumbled on top of canned or fresh fruit then cooked in the oven to make a crumble. Or cut the cake up, and layer it with custard and Jell-O, adding a good splash of sherry every now and then to make a trifle.

✔ Old, hard cheese is fine in cheese sauce.

✔ Leftover veggies make excellent soup. Just boil them in broth and purée.

✔ Put leftover veggies in quiche — any type will do!

✔ Top leftover anything (chicken, veggies, meat) with cheese sauce and place a piece of pre-rolled pasty cut to size on top, or use crumbled stale bread. Bake in a hot oven till golden brown for a delicious pie.

Emergency Eating

You've spent all your money again, and now you're home and hungry and there's nothing to eat. What can you do?

- Go to a restaurant where you only pay as much as you can afford. You'll find them all over. For example, there's *Same cafe* in Denver, Colorado, or *Soul Kitchen* in, Red Bank, NJ, as well as *Panera Cares* cafes all around the place. Don't give much money this time, but for good karma, make sure you go back and pay more next time when you have the cash.

- Find a soup kitchen — you might feel embarrassed, but everyone has a time when they need a helping hand. Google *soup kitchen* and your city.

- Do some volunteer work — apart from being good for your soul, you will often get fed. And how great will you feel?

- Whatever your feelings about religion, go to church or the synagogue — there are often refreshments afterwards, and they may be able to point you in the right direction for other cheap food options. Some places run food programs themselves, and you could either use the services offered or offer to help out and you'll be sure to get a meal. And you might just enjoy it anyway.

- Keep an eye out in the local paper, and find a focus group. It won't help you today, but you will find that in exchange for your opinions, you are usually fed as well as being paid. And it can be fun to know what different organizations are planning.

- Attend free events (such as lectures or concerts) that include refreshments. There are lots around — you just need to track them down. Look at your local paper, or keep an eye on community noticeboards.

- Go to your local food market at closing time to pick up some bargains — the sellers don't really want to have to pack up their perishable food to take home.

- Barter with your friends and neighbors — perhaps you could swap your herbs for their lemons.

- Try local bakeries at the very end of the day — they don't mind getting rid of today's bread very cheaply as they can't easily sell it the next day.

- And finally, visit members of your family! (Okay, maybe a last resort, but along with an earful about how you need to plan better, you'll get a free meal.)

Barter with your friends and neighbors

Five Top Tips

1. Immediately wipe up any spills on the stove, or in the pantry or refrigerator — they're so much harder to clean up once they set and are even worse if they are cooked on.

2. Shop at the supermarket. It's not very chic, but their turnover is high and their prices are low, so you can be pretty sure of getting reasonable produce at a reasonable price. And if not, they will take it back.

3. For better taste, nutrition, and cost, buy food when it's in season and preferably grown locally. And buy things on special if you can store them and know you'll use them.

4. To minimize the chance of food poisoning, don't mix raw and cooked foods, and keep chicken, seafood, egg dishes, and dairy well chilled. Don't leave them out on the countertop.

5. Go to the store when you have just eaten, keeping to a list and spending only up to the amount allocated in your budget. All these things will help keep your finances under control.

CHAPTER 5

What's For Dinner?

It's 6:30 p.m. You've just walked in the door from work, and you quickly realize there's no mom cooking dinner for you. Unless you're a serious fan of Cheerios or have the budget and waistline that can cope with eating out every night, here are a few recipes that will happily keep body and soul together.

Haven't Got Time to Read the Whole Chapter? Read This.

1. If you're starving and want to eat in the next 20 minutes or so, cook an omelet (five minutes), a stir fry (10 minutes), risotto (15 minutes), or some soup (20 minutes). All are faster than jumping in your car and eating out.

2. Nothing in the fridge but a few old veggies? Make soup! You can put almost anything in with some stock (as long as it's edible) and cook it up, and it will taste fine.

3. You can make a quick lasagna with just leftover Bolognaise sauce, grated cheese, and lasagna noodles. Alternate the layers, stick it in the oven, and you're done.

4. Make a batch of cookie dough, and freeze it. You can make cookies at the snap of a finger. What a star!

5. To test if a cake is done, gently touch the top with your finger — it should bounce back and feel dry if the cake's ready to come out of the oven. Check by inserting a skewer into the middle of the cake, and if it comes out clean, the cake is ready.

Soup Recipes

Soup is great — it's healthy and cheap, you can use whatever you have in the refrigerator, and it's really quick and easy to make. Oh, and it's delicious too! If you're not a soupy-type person, give it a try. You never know — you might be converted.

Basic veggie soup

INGREDIENTS

About 3 cups of chopped vegetables, whatever you feel like or is in season

1 onion, chopped

Butter or cooking spray

Broth or a bouillon cube + water

Bacon, chopped (optional)

Herbs, washed and chopped (optional)

Pepper and salt

METHOD

In a saucepan, heat up the butter and oil together and gently fry the vegetables and onion, as well as the bacon, and herbs if using, for around 10 minutes. Add broth (or use a bouillon cube and water, 1 cube for every 1 cup of water) to cover the veggies and simmer (gently boil) for another 15 minutes or until the veggies are soft. Purée if you like. Add pepper and, if needed, salt.

Some other good combinations include:

Bacon and corn soup

Fry up a couple of chopped strips of bacon and a chopped onion, add 4 chopped potatoes, 1 cup milk, 4 cups of broth, and a ½ teaspoon of dried thyme, and boil gently till the veggies are all soft. Add a can of creamed corn, and blend till smooth.

Best ever roast veggie soup

Boil up leftover roast veggies (carrot, sweet potato, potato, onion) in broth till soft, and then purée. Magnificent!

Broccoli (and blue cheese) soup

Gently fry up the stalk and florets of broccoli then cover with chicken broth and simmer as above. Once ready, add some blue cheese if you wish and purée.

Curried cauliflower soup

Cook up the stalk and florets of cauliflower, a chopped onion, and a few good shakes of curry powder (or a teaspoon of curry paste) in butter or oil as above, and then add chicken broth to cover. Simmer as above. Purée.

Lentil soup

Fry a chopped onion in a little oil, and add a can of tomatoes and ¾ cup dried lentils (any color). Add beef broth to cover, then simmer for 15 minutes or until lentils are soft.

Zucchini soup

Cut up some zucchini and onion, and fry in a little oil. If desired, cook a couple of chopped strips of bacon as well. Add broth to cover the veggies, simmer until they are soft, and then purée.

Sauce Recipes

Sauces can be great for dressing up a simple meal — pour a mushroom sauce over steak or pasta or how about a cheese sauce over macaroni? Start with a Béchamel (white sauce) and move on from there.

White sauce (Béchamel)

INGREDIENTS

2 oz. butter
⅓ cup all-purpose flour
4 cups milk
Pepper and salt
A pinch of nutmeg

METHOD

Melt the butter in a saucepan over medium heat then add the flour and stir to make a thick paste. Continue to cook this for two minutes, stirring all the time, until it is bubbling; then take it off the heat. Pour in the milk, little by little, whisking all the while. Once it's all incorporated and smooth, put it back on the heat and bring to a boil while stirring. The sauce is ready once it thickens and coats the back of the spoon.

Cheese sauce

Take your white sauce off the heat and add a good handful of grated Parmesan cheese or tasty cheese (or live on the wild side and add both) and half a teaspoon of mustard from a jar to give it a kick. Stir it well till the cheese melts then add pepper and, if needed, salt.

Mushroom sauce

Fry sliced mushrooms in a little butter and add to your white sauce at the end. Some port wine, soy sauce, and dried dill can turn it into a gourmet treat.

Tomato pasta sauce

For a simple tomato pasta sauce, fry up a chopped onion and some crushed garlic in a little oil, add half a teaspoon of dried herbs or a few chopped fresh herbs of your choice, and then add a can of diced tomatoes. Bring to a boil and simmer for 5 minutes. A splash of red wine and a small amount of sugar will bring out the flavor. You can purée this or leave it chunky.

Recipes with Meat

A general cooking guide

Sometimes when you're at the grocery store looking at the rows of vegetables or the shelves of meat, it can be hard to imagine how you will cook them all. What type of meat do I need for a stir-fry? What goes well in a casserole? Here's a guide to help you out.

Pan fry or BBQ/grill

You can use a range of cuts of chicken and beef, as well as diced chicken threaded on a bamboo skewer. Any type of steak is a good choice. You can cook these alongside sliced potatoes (pre-cooked is best), zucchini, onion, eggplant, and mushrooms. Then serve them with a salad or steamed veggies.

Roasts

One of the easiest things to cook is a roast, whether it's a whole chicken or beef roast, or even pork or lamb. You can roast an array of veggies, including beetroot, garlic, carrots, eggplant, parsnip, potatoes, sweet potatoes, and zucchini.

One of the easiest things to cook is a roast

Stir-fry

Good meat choices include sliced chicken and any type of sliced steak. You can cook these with a variety of sliced or diced vegetables, including onion, garlic, Asian vegetables, cauliflower, broccoli, peas, green beans, cabbage, carrot, zucchini, peppers, and bean shoots.

Casserole or slow cooker

You need meat that responds to a long, slow cook, such as chicken pieces or a whole chicken, or a cheaper cut of beef. Harder veggies such as potato, carrots, and onions can go in at the start, and softer ones such as zucchini, mushrooms, peas, and sweet potato can go closer towards the end.

Cooking Steak

If you're short on time, a steak can be a quick "go to" meal. To cook a perfect steak, first heat the frying pan or BBQ/grill to medium. The steak should sizzle as it makes contact with the heat. Minimize how often you turn it over; if you keep flipping it, it will get tough. When moisture comes to the surface, turn it over.

Touch the surface of your steak using your tongs — if it's very soft. it's rare. If it's firm, it's well done. Yep, if it's in between, it's medium-rare. Over time, you'll work out which "feel" corresponds with each level of "doneness." Don't forget about residual heat. Your steak will keep cooking once you take it off the heat, so cook slightly less rather than slightly more.

Resting your meat

One thing to note is that all meat needs time to rest before serving. It will lose less juice when cut and will therefore be more succulent and tastier. Covering it in aluminum foil can stop it from cooling down too much. The bigger the piece of meat, the longer it needs to rest: between a couple of minutes for a steak or piece of chicken and up to 15 minutes for a roast.

All meat needs time to rest before serving

Which brings me to…

Roast recipes

A roast will generally be cooked in a moderate oven for 30 minutes per pound of weight at around 375°F. So if you are a math genius like me, you will able to work out that a three-pound chicken roast will require 1½ hours. Generally, you can just throw a roast in a roasting pan and then into a pre-heated oven and forget about it. Put some peeled potatoes, sweet potatoes, or onions around the bottom of the pan with some oil, turn them every now and then, and that's your veggies done too.

You should always make sure that chicken is cooked, so stick a knife in to the fleshy part of the drumstick — if the juices run clear, it is cooked, but if they are still bloody, it needs slightly longer.

Make sure you take the meat out of the roasting pan to let it rest before serving, and then you can turn up the temperature to crisp the veggies for that last 15 minutes.

Lemon-up-the-bottom chicken

If you want something a little more gourmet than a standard roast, how about a lemon-up-the-bottom chicken? Delicious AND a conversation starter!

INGREDIENTS

1 chicken

2 lemons

Freshly ground black pepper

METHOD

- Heat the oven to 375°F. Get a fork, and poke deep holes in the lemons all over. Check that there is nothing in the chicken's cavity (such as stuffing or the neck) — if there is, remove it. Push the lemons up the chicken's bottom. Grind lots of pepper all over the chicken.

- Put a very small amount of butter or water in the bottom of the roasting pan, or put the chicken on a roasting rack in the pan so that the chicken doesn't stick. Roast for 1–1½ hours or until, when you insert a knife near the joint of the leg, the juices run clear, not red. Spooning up the juices and pouring them over the chicken while it cooks (i.e., basting) will give you a crispier skin.

Honey soy chicken

This is a great dish that only takes seconds to prepare and then less than an hour in the oven to cook. And it's delicious too!

INGREDIENTS

⅓ cup honey

⅔ cup soy sauce

One clove garlic, crushed

A squeeze of lemon if you want

8 chicken drumsticks (or use diced chicken or chicken thighs for a change)

METHOD

Place the chicken in an ovenproof dish. Mix the other ingredients together and pour over the chicken; then bake at 375°F for 45 minutes, turning every 15 minutes and spooning the sauce over. The chicken is cooked if juices run clear when you pierce the thickest part of the chicken with a knife or skewer.

Chicken Curry

There's not much better than a good chicken curry. Except another good chicken curry! Because this recipe

Green curry is hotter than red

uses coconut milk, you would traditionally use a Thai curry paste rather than Indian, but go ahead and use what you want. If you do use a Thai curry, remember that green curry is hotter than red - who knew?

INGREDIENTS

2 chicken breasts diced into chunks

Approx. 1 tablespoon curry paste (more or less according to how hot you like your curry)

2 cups of canned coconut milk

Your pick of veggies, such as green beans, snow peas, broccoli, mushrooms, peas—chopped or diced if they are large

1 garlic clove

2 tablespoons oil

METHOD

Heat the oil in a frying pan, add the garlic, and stir for one minute, then add the chicken and lightly brown it all over. Add the curry paste and, if it's looking dry, a dash of oil; then stir for 30 seconds. Add the coconut milk, and bring to a boil; then decrease the heat and gently simmer for around 15 minutes till the chicken is cooked through. Finally add the veggies for the last 5 minutes till they are cooked but still crunchy. Serve with jasmine (fragrant) rice.

Maple mustard chicken

There is a rumor out there that this is the best recipe in the world. I'm almost convinced it's true, but even if it's not, it is definitely delicious and very, very easy.

INGREDIENTS

8 chicken thighs (or use cut-up breast if you want, but this won't be as moist)

¼ cup maple syrup (use the real thing, not pancake syrup)

½ cup smooth, mild mustard such as Dijon

1½ tablespoon white wine vinegar

1½ teaspoons chopped rosemary

2 garlic cloves, crushed

Salt & pepper

METHOD

Put the chicken in a large baking dish. Put all the other ingredients on top and swirl them all around to mix everything together. Bake at 450°F for around 35 minutes until the chicken is cooked. (This recipe was adapted from *nerdswithknives*.[7])

Meatloaf

So easy ! So economical! So tasty! It's a winner all around.

Meatloaf is a winner all round

INGREDIENTS

1½ lbs. ground beef (low fat if your budget is up to it)

1 carrot and 1 zucchini, both grated

⅓ cup tomato ketchup

1½ cups breadcrumbs made from fresh bread (just grate it up yourself)

2 eggs

A few shakes of dried mixed herbs (whatever you have in the pantry) or some chopped fresh ones

METHOD

Mix everything in a large bowl. (Go on — get your hands in there! They're much more efficient than a wooden spoon.) Put it all into a greased, deep and rectangular loaf tin, and bake at 375°F for around 45 minutes or until cooked. Check it from 30 minutes onwards to avoid it being overdone. If you feel like dressing it up, you can fry up some chopped bacon and onion and add them in with all the other ingredients at the very start. Serve with mashed potatoes, a green veggie, and some extra ketchup.

Stir-fry

If you are really short on time, a stir-fry is an excellent solution. You can have this on the table in less than 10 minutes. And it won't break the bank.

INGREDIENTS

Strips of meat—any type will do

Prepared veggies chopped into manageable pieces. The only exception is garlic, which you should crush.

Oil

Some type of liquid: soy sauce, broth, or purchased stir-fry sauce

METHOD

Heat a tablespoon of oil in a wok or high-sided frying pan, throw in the strips of meat, and fry for a couple of minutes, stirring continuously till they are lightly browned. If you are using onion or garlic, put them in and fry them for a minute or so, adding a teaspoon of oil if required. Now throw in the rest of the veggies, again adding a teaspoon of oil if required, and fry for a couple of minutes. (You can take the meat out and cook the vegetables by themselves to avoid overcooking the meat and then add it back in with the sauce, but I tend to just leave it in there.)

Try a piece of vegetable to check if they are done, and when they are, add in one of the following:

- A couple of shakes of soy sauce and a tablespoon of honey, if you feel like it
- ½ cup of broth (or ½ cup water with ½ a bouillon cube dissolved in it)
- A jar or pack of purchased stir-fry sauce

Keep stirring for a minute or so till it's all hot, and serve. Eat with rice, potatoes, flat bread, or pasta. You can throw the rice, potatoes, or pasta (all cooked) into the wok near the end if you like.

Pasta Recipes

Spaghetti Bolognaise

You've probably been eating Spaghetti Bolognaise since you were a little kid, and this is why: it's delicious, it's quick, it's cheap, and it's reasonably healthy. Here's a recipe, but if you're really short on time, don't be ashamed to buy one of those jars of pasta sauces designed to be added to meat. If you do, you'll just need to fry some ground beef till it's lightly brown, breaking it up with the wooden spoon as you go along. Add the bottled sauce, some wine if you like, and some grated veggies or red lentils, and then cook it all up and enjoy. Lentils in particular are a great addition as they give you more volume and increase the protein level. And they're cheap too.

But if you've got the time, here's a basic Bolognaise recipe to make from scratch. Go for it!

Basic Spaghetti Bolognaise

Don't be afraid to make this a day or two in advance as it gets better and better. Some "flaveur de refrigerator" can work wonders.

Make spaghetti bolognaise a day or two in advance

INGREDIENTS

1 lb. ground beef (choose the low fat one if you can afford it)

1 onion, chopped

2 garlic cloves, crushed

1 carrot, grated

1 zucchini, grated

½ cup red wine

1 teaspoon of Italian herbs (or just oregano if you prefer)

½ tablespoon of sugar if required (taste first; depends on the ripeness of the tomatoes)

3 tablespoons of tomato paste, or tomato ketchup if that's all you've got

1 can of chopped tomatoes

Optional: ½ cup red lentils and/or 3 strips of bacon, chopped

METHOD

Fry up the bacon (if using) for a couple of minutes, then add the onion and garlic. Fry for a couple more minutes but don't let them brown; then add the meat and fry until it's brown. As you do so, break up the meat with a wooden spoon. Add all the other ingredients and some more liquid if it's looking too dry. This can be plain water, beef broth, or water and a beef bouillon cube. Boil for as long as you've got — anywhere from five minutes on medium heat to an hour on very low is fine. Serve with any type of pasta and lots of grated Parmesan cheese.

Easy lasagna

Make a big batch of Bolognaise sauce and use it the next day to make a lasagna! This recipe doesn't require you to make a cheesy sauce, so it's very easy, but if you're in a kitchen groove, make the cheese sauce mentioned earlier instead.

INGREDIENTS

Bolognaise sauce

Lasagna pasta

Grated cheese (or cheese sauce)

METHOD

Fill a large rectangular dish starting with a smear of meat sauce to stop sticking, then a layer of lasagna pasta, followed by a layer of meat sauce, and then a sprinkling of cheese. Repeat the pasta, sauce and cheese layers until you either fill the dish or run out of one of the ingredients, but make sure your last layer is pasta topped with sprinkled cheese. Cook in a pre-heated 375°F oven for around 30 minutes till the top is golden brown and crunchy. Serve with lettuce and tomato and perhaps some crunchy bread.

Egg Recipes

Spaghetti Carbonara

A good Spaghetti Carbonara is hard to beat, and it's a delicious meal when you don't have much in the cupboard. I've been making this for years, tweaked from an original recipe by Guy Grossi.

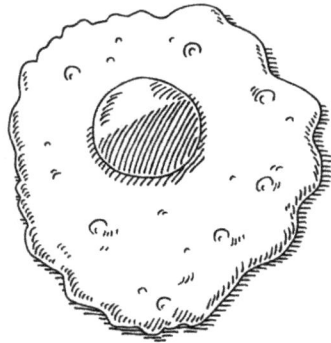

INGREDIENTS

5 oz. pancetta or bacon (can be replaced with ham if that's all you've got)

5 eggs, whisked with a fork

Pepper and salt

2 good handfuls of grated Parmesan cheese

4 tablespoons of chopped parsley

Spaghetti

METHOD

- Cut up the pancetta into pieces and fry in a deep frying pan. Meanwhile, cook the spaghetti according to the instructions on the pack. Once the pancetta is golden brown, turn off the heat. In a separate bowl, break in the eggs and mix in the chopped parsley and most of the Parmesan cheese, leaving some to sprinkle on the top at the end. Season with pepper and salt.

- Once the spaghetti is cooked, drain it and return it to the hot pan; then quickly add in the pancetta and the egg mixture. Stir. The residual heat of the pasta will cook the egg slightly and form the sauce. (Look! It's magic!) If it's too cold and the egg is not cooking, you can pop it back on the stovetop and stir over low heat for 30 seconds or so. Sprinkle with Parmesan cheese.

Quiche Lorraine

A quiche takes only minutes to prepare and an hour to cook; a homemade quiche will beat a store-bought one every time, and they are so easy to make you should try to resist the temptation to buy one. Really — trust me on this! Great served warm with a salad for dinner or cold for lunch or a picnic.

INGREDIENTS

Pastry—either make your own (see below) or use a commercial pie crust mix (follow the instructions on the pack)

3 eggs

A couple of slices of bacon (leave these out if they're not your style)

4 slices of Swiss cheese (for a traditional quiche) or a big handful of grated tasty cheese

1 cup milk

½ cup fresh cream

A pinch of nutmeg

Salt and pepper

METHOD – PASTRY

- <u>Making your own:</u> Mix 1 cup all-purpose flour, 2 oz. of butter (softened), a pinch of salt, and a pinch of baking powder in a blender until it looks like breadcrumbs. If you don't have a blender, you can use your fingertips to mix it in a bowl. Add an egg yolk, a squeeze of lemon, and 1 tablespoon of water. Blend again (or use your hands), adding more water if necessary till it comes together in a ball. Put in the refrigerator for 20 minutes then roll out and line the pie plate.

<u>Using pie crust mix:</u> If you are using a commercial mix, follow the instructions on the side of the box. But personally, I think it's as easy to make your own, and I know you're smart enough!

METHOD – FILLING

- Heat the oven to 400°F.

- Cut off the excess pastry level with the top of the pie dish, and place the dish in the refrigerator for around 20 minutes.

- Meanwhile, if you are using bacon, chop it into small pieces and fry (it won't need fat). In a bowl, mix your eggs, milk, cream, nutmeg, salt, and pepper. Take out two tablespoons of this mix, and put it into a mug with a tablespoon of flour. Stir this till it's smooth, and then put it back into the bowl it came from and stir well.

- Put the cooked bacon, if using, on the bottom of the pie dish and then the cheese. Put the pie plate on a baking tray, pour in the egg mixture, and cook in the oven for 15 minutes; then turn the oven down to 375°F and cook until the top is lightly brown and the mixture is set, around 45 minutes.

A quiche takes only minutes to prepare

- Delicious!

Other quiches

For variations, add any of the following:

- Defrosted frozen spinach (squeeze it out well over the sink)
- Some gently fried, sliced leek. Wash it well before frying as it can be gritty.

- Canned salmon or tuna, drained
- Leftover chopped up veggies
- Feta cheese instead of the Gruyère or tasty cheese
- Caramelized onion with goat's cheese (leave out the other cheese)
- Anything you've ever tried in a quiche before! Just make sure it's not too wet and you put it in the pastry flan before you put in the milk and egg mix.

Omelets

An omelet has to be about the quickest meal you can make, and it's delicious.

INGREDIENTS
2 eggs
½ tablespoon water
Cooking spray

METHOD

- Break 2 eggs into a cup, and add the water. Mix this up with a fork. Spray a frying pan with oil, and heat it up till it's medium hot. Pour in the eggs, and swirl them around the frying pan till they cover the base. Using the side of a fork, push from the outside edge to the center, and then tilt the pan towards that spot, allowing the mixture to fill the part of the saucepan that is now bare. Do this four or five times.
- Turn to medium, and allow it to cook for about 2 minutes. (The water you've added into the eggs will turn into steam, fluffing up the omelet). Add chopped cheese, ham, thinly sliced veggies, or anything you like onto the top of half the omelet, and leave for another minute or so. Fold the empty half of the omelet over the top of the half with things on top, and then slide it onto a plate to serve.

Rice Recipes

Risotto

You must use Arborio rice to make risotto

Risotto is another great dish to prepare — quick, cheap, and can be made with whatever you've got on hand in your cupboard. However, you must use Arborio rice, which has a high starch content and can absorb masses of liquid to become deliciously creamy but not soggy. Another tip is that if it's available, buy a block of ungrated Parmesan cheese and grate it yourself.

INGREDIENTS

3 oz. Arborio rice per person

One teaspoon of butter per person

1¼ cups liquid (just broth by itself or a mix of broth and wine) per person

Parmesan cheese

METHOD

- Heat up your broth/wine mix in a saucepan till it is just simmering, and keep it gently bubbling while you are making the risotto. Put the rice and butter into a saucepan and cook, stirring, till the rice is glossy and translucent. Not too long! Ladle half a cup of broth into the rice mixture, and stir while it bubbles away. Once it's all been absorbed, add some more liquid and stir again. Repeat till all the broth is gone.

- Stir in a good handful of Parmesan cheese and any herbs you might have on hand. Sprinkle with Parmesan to serve.

There is not much you can't add into your risotto. Here are are a couple of ideas to try:

- ½ teaspoon of saffron and some chopped onion — fry the onion with the rice, and add the saffron half way through the ladling process (this one's called Risotto Milanese).

- Smoked salmon, capers, and lemon juice — put in a minute or so before the end, and don't stir too vigorously or you'll mash the salmon.

- Asparagus, peas, and lemon juice — cook the asparagus before adding all ingredients a minute or so before the end.

- Tomato and ham. Simple but delicious.

Fried rice

This is another great classic that doesn't take long to prepare, is cheap and, depending on what you add into it, can be nutritious

INGREDIENTS

Leftover cooked rice (or cook some early in the day and leave it to cool in the refrigerator)

Soy Sauce

Oil

Any of the following:

- Chopped veggies (those frozen chopped ones in a bag are good or anything else you've got on hand)
- Tomato
- Sliced lettuce (yes, weird, but delicious!)
- Egg
- Bacon
- Onion
- Garlic (crushed)
- Cooked shrimp, chicken, or pork in small pieces

METHOD

Heat up some oil in your large frying pan; add the onion, garlic, bacon, or veggies and cook, stirring. Move these to the side of the pan, and pour in the egg that you have whisked with a fork in a cup. Cook it in one piece, turn it over with your slotted turner, and when it is cooked, cut it through using the edge of your turner. (You should end up with little ribbons of egg, but it doesn't matter what you end up with actually!) Add in the rice, splash on soy sauce until you've got some color, and mix everything through together. Cook for another minute or so till the whole dish is hot, and serve.

Making Cakes

Everyone should know how to whip up a good cake. Once you get the hang of them, cakes only take about 5 minutes to prepare, and you can have one ready (well, at least in the oven) from the time someone says they're coming to visit till when they ring the doorbell.

Checklist: Cake tips

✔ Use eggs at room temperature, not from the refrigerator — you'll get a bigger volume when you beat them, resulting in a lighter cake.

✔ Often recipes will ask you to cream together the butter and sugar, which means beating them together until the mixture is light in color and creamy in texture. You then beat in the eggs and fold in the flour and milk alternately. This is the correct way to make a cake, and it will give a great texture, but we're talking easy here, so you can cheat by just melting the butter in a cup and beating it with the other ingredients.

✔ You can then use the leftover butter in the cup to paint around the pan with a pastry brush so the cake doesn't stick. If the pan's not made of silicone, line the base with a circle of parchment paper as well.

✔ If you are using a convection oven, drop the temperature by 50°F from what's stated in the recipe.

✔ Cook cakes as close to the middle of the oven as you can, and turn the pans around when the cake is set (about ⅔ of the way through the cooking time).

✔ At the end of the cooking time, and if you think the cake might be ready, touch the top of the cake gently. If it's cooked, your finger will bounce back, and the cake won't feel gooey. The cake also won't wobble as you slide the rack out of the oven.

✔ If it feels dry and there's no wobbling, insert a skewer into the cake. If there is goo on the bottom of the skewer when you pull it out, stick the cake back into the oven for another 10 minutes or so and then repeat the skewer action. The skewer will come out clean when the cake is cooked.

Issues with cakes

PROBLEM	CAUSE
Cake splits during cooking	• The oven is too hot
Cake doesn't rise	• The oven is too cool, or • The recipe is wrong (maybe not enough baking powder)
Cake rises then sinks	• The cake hasn't been cooked long enough, or • There's too much baking powder • You opened the oven half way and the temperature dropped suddenly ☹

Cake Recipes

The easiest cake is the famous (at least in our family) Throw It All In & Stir chocolate cake.

Throw It All In and Stir chocolate cake

This recipe has been in my family for generations. It can be adapted to make a whole range of cakes, and the best part is that there is no one who can't make it.

INGREDIENTS

1 cup sugar

1 cup all-purpose flour

2 teaspoons baking powder

½ teaspoon salt

½ cup milk

2 tablespoons cocoa

3 tablespoons butter, melted in a cup in the microwave

2 eggs

1 teaspoon vanilla (essence, extract, whatever you have)

METHOD

- First heat the oven to 350°F. Throw all the ingredients together into a bowl. Stir vigorously by hand (or with a mixer) till the mixture gets thicker and lighter in color. Sometimes, because of kitchen gremlins, it doesn't, and that's fine. Sit your silicone cake pan on an oven tray, and brush the pan with the leftover butter in the cup, or spray with a nonstick cooking spray like Baker's Joy or Pam with Flour. If you are using a metal cake pan, cut out a circle of parchment paper to sit on the bottom, and paint the sides with the leftover butter or spray as above

- Cook for about 45 minutes or until a skewer inserted into the middle comes out clean. If there is goo on the bottom of the skewer, stick the cake back into the oven for another 10 minutes or so and repeat the skewer action. You can also touch the top of the cake gently, and you'll feel if it's cooked – it shouldn't be gooey at all, and there should be no wobbling.

- Once it's cooked, leave the cake in the pan for 5 minutes; then carefully run a blunt knife around the edge, put a wire cooling rack on top, and flip it over so that the cake is now upside down on the rack. Remove the pan. Be careful as it's all very fragile at this stage. After another 10 minutes, put a plate upside down on the bottom of the cake, and flip the whole thing back up the right way so the cake is now on the plate. Sift powdered sugar on the top. Impressive!

Pudding cake

Simply replace the cocoa with a 4 oz. pack of instant pudding mix (any flavor). Cook as above. This makes a really dense and delicious cake. If you really want to go all out, add in a pack of chocolate chips at the stirring stage — chocolate ones for a (you guessed it!) chocolate cake and white ones for any other flavor.

Orange cake

Leave out the cocoa and add in the grated rind of one orange. Instead of the ½ cup of milk, use ¼ cup milk and ¼ cup orange juice.

Cinnamon apple cake

Leave out the cocoa, and place peeled, cored, and finely sliced apple decoratively on the top. Once it's cooked and out of the oven, brush with a little melted butter then sprinkle with 1 tablespoon of granulated sugar mixed with a couple of good shakes of cinnamon.

Coffee cake

Leave out the cocoa. When it's hot out of the oven, spread with melted butter and sprinkle with 1 tablespoon of granulated sugar mixed with a couple of good shakes of cinnamon.

Banana cake

If Maple Syrup Chicken is the king of savory recipes, then this Banana Cake is the queen of sweet ones. It's sensational! To make it, leave out the cocoa and increase the flour to 1¾ cups. Blend all ingredients with 2 sliced bananas and 1 teaspoon baking soda. Some people have been known to mix in a handful of chocolate chips after blending, but really! Wouldn't you rather eat the chocolate chips while you wait for the cake to bake? I would.

Cupcakes

Use 1½ cups of all-purpose flour instead of 1 cup. Spoon into the holes of a muffin tin that have been brushed with butter. Cook until golden brown and a skewer inserted comes out clean.

Frosting

If it's for a special occasion, you can decorate your cake quickly and easily with this frosting.

INGREDIENTS

A generous tablespoon of butter

2 cups powdered sugar, sifted

Enough milk to make a spreadable paste

Coloring

Decorate a cake with frosting and top with a fresh flower. Very Master Chef!

METHOD

- Put the butter into a bowl and melt it in the microwave. Add the powdered sugar. Mix, adding milk tablespoon by tablespoon until you get to a spreadable consistency (similar to toothpaste).

- If you want to have colored frosting, add a few drops of coloring now and mix well. If you want to make pink frosting, use only a very little butter at the start, as otherwise it will end up being orange!

- Spread this on a COOL cake, starting at the middle of the top and working out toward the edges. You can go down the sides if you have enough frosting and are feeling extravagant. If you put frosting on a hot cake, it will all melt and run onto the plate. So sad.

- A fresh-cut flower on top looks very *Master Chef*, or you can even just add some candles if it's for a birthday.

Pancakes

Weird, but if you want to make pancakes, just add an extra teaspoon of baking powder to the **Throw It All In & Stir** mixture, and leave out the cocoa. (Buy hey, if you want chocolate pancakes, leave it in!) Spray your large frying pan with oil or use melted butter. Pour on the mixture to make the size pancake you want, and flip when there are bubbles all the way through and the edge of the pancake is dry. Cook only half a minute or so on the other side.

If you are after French-style crepes, use more milk and less flour to get a thinner batter. Pour in just enough to enable you to swirl it around over the bottom of the pan in a very thin layer. After a minute or so, peek under the edge to see if it's brown, and then slide a spatula underneath and flip it over to the other side and cook for about 20 seconds.

The first pancake is always a mess — supposedly you're meant to give it to the hens to say thank you for the eggs (but the dog will be happy to oblige).

Cookie Recipes

There's really only one cookie that we need to include here. Not very complicated but oh so delicious! Although I'm not sure it's possible, if you end up making too much dough, you can freeze it. Then, when you're short of time and need some cookies, just cut it into slices while frozen, place on a tray, and throw in the oven. Easy.

Chocolate chip cookies

INGREDIENTS
4½ oz. butter
½ cup sugar
½ cup brown sugar
1 teaspoon vanilla
1 egg

½ cup quick oats

1½ cups all-purpose flour

2 teaspoons baking powder

½ teaspoon salt

4½ oz. chocolate chips (white, milk, dark, or a mixture) or chopped up bits of leftover chocolate

METHOD

- Heat the oven to 375°F. Beat the butter, sugars, and vanilla together by hand or with a mixer till the mixture is smooth; then add the egg and beat again. Don't worry if it curdles and looks lumpy. Stir in the flour, quick oats, and salt, and finally mix in the chocolate chips. This step will be tricky as the mixture will be firm.

- Form into balls slightly smaller than the size cookie you want, and place them on a baking tray lined with parchment paper. Leave a gap between them as they will spread.

- Bake for about 12–15 minutes, until they are golden brown and the top of each cookie is slightly set. Make sure they are still soft as cookies continue to firm up as they cool and what looks like a great texture in the oven can become rock hard once they're cold. After 5 minutes out of the oven, use a turner or spatula to gently lift them and place them on a cooling rack to firm up.

For those of you who really want some variations, here are two:

Plain cookies

You can leave out the chocolate chips, but really, have you thought this through? Decorate the top with half a maraschino cherry. Or instead of the cherries, once cool, dip half of each cookie in melted chocolate. Leave to set on a piece of parchment paper.

Fruit cookies

Use raisins or chopped up dried apricots instead of the chocolate chips.

Five Top Tips

1. Make sure you rest your meat when it comes out of the oven or off the grill. It will be more tender and juicy.

2. All you have to do to cook a roast is put it in the oven for 30 minutes per 1 pound of weight at 375°F. Nothing hard about that.

3. If your cake splits when cooking, the oven was too hot. If it sinks when it comes out of the oven, it wasn't cooked long enough. And if it's flat, you either didn't put in enough baking powder or the oven was too cold.

4. Make sure that cookies come out of the oven while they are still soft. Remember that they harden up on cooling, so a really soft cookie in the oven can become rock hard once cold.

5. Eggs make an excellent meal that is quick, healthy and cheap. Try an omelet, a quiche, a soufflé, or even a boiled or scrambled egg. Delicious!

CHAPTER 6

I Don't Feel So Well ...

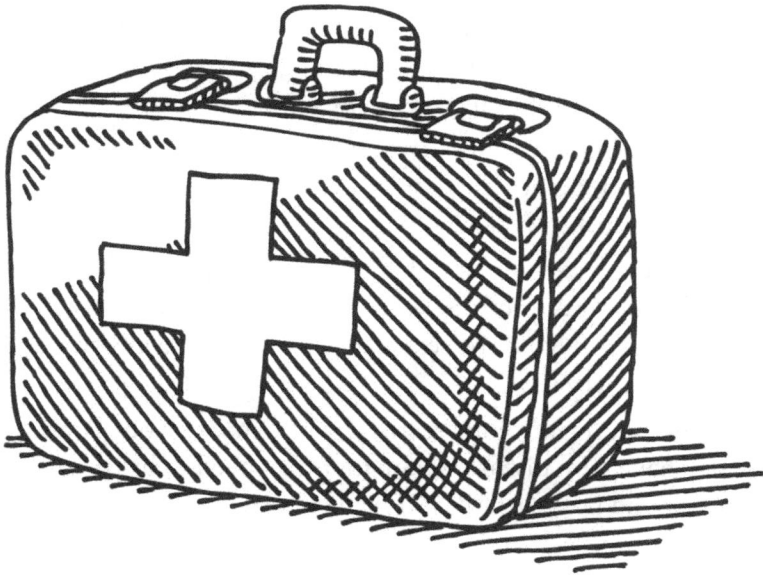

Now that you are out on your own and don't have your mom nagging you ("Have you had your breakfast?" "What time did you get to bed last night?" "Are you eating enough fruit and vegetables?"), perhaps it's time that you started thinking seriously about your own health. The little things you do every day can make a big difference overall as to how well you feel and how much you can achieve in your day-to-day life. So sit back and relax, and read on to find out how you can manage your own health.

Haven't Got Time to Read the Whole Chapter? Read This.

1. If you're feeling sad or anxious or think you may have an eating disorder, seek help early. Don't worry — just go online to *NAMI* (for mental health information and support), *ADAA* (Anxiety and Depression Association of America), or *NEDA* (National Eating Disorders Association). It's free, and you can remain anonymous if you want.

2. Keep healthy by having 150 minutes of exercise per week, eating lean meat and lots of fruit and veggies, and drinking water in preference to anything else.

3. RICE is the best way to treat a sprain: Rest, Ice, Compression, and Elevation. If there is severe pain, bruising, or loss of function, see your doctor.

4. Sixty-seven percent of chlamydia cases reported each year are in the age group of 15- to 24-year-olds.[8] Even if you have no symptoms, if you are sexually active, do a urine test at your doctor's every year.

5. When you brush your teeth, if what you spit out is pink, you may have gum disease (gingivitis). You need to brush your teeth better and floss every day. If it continues, see your dentist.

A Healthy Lifestyle

Did you know that scientists have discovered burgers and fries are a healthy diet? Nah, just kidding.

Sadly, the truth is that you need to do the following to keep healthy:[9]

- Get 150 minutes of moderate exercise each week[10]. Something that gets you huffing and puffing is good, but whatever you enjoy doing is fine as long as it's active. Twice a week you should also do some strength training.

- Eat lean meat, chicken and fish, tofu, nuts, legumes, and eggs (5½ oz. a day).

- Eat lean dairy products (3 cups a day).

- Have lots of different colored veggies (2½ cups a day) and fruits (2 cups a day).

- Eat wholegrain carbohydrates & cereals (6 oz. a day).

- Eat oily fish, which is high in Omega-3 fatty acids. Oily fish includes salmon, sardines, tuna, mackerel, and anchovies, and these are great fresh or from a can.

- Drink water over soda or fruit juices. Tap water is perfect.

- Don't drink too much alcohol (up to one standard drink for women and two standard drinks for men per day). A standard drink is defined as one shot of 80% liquor, a 5 fluid oz. glass of wine, or a 12 fluid oz. can of beer.[11] Of course, if you're under 21, this book is not advocating that you drink at all. ☺

- Limit salty foods, saturated fats, trans fats and sugar.

Get 150 minutes of moderate exercise each week

Are you at risk from a weight-related health issue? According to the International Diabetes Federation,[12] one way to know is to grab a tape measure and put it around your waist — if your waist is over 31.5" (as a woman) or 35.5" (as a man), you may be.

It's not unusual to put on weight once you leave home

It's not unusual to put on weight once you leave the confines of home, so if this is a problem for you, look at the *Beating the Freshman 15* website.[13] But remember — we're talking about health here and not about trying to look like someone in the media. Love yourself, don't compare yourself to others, and do things that you enjoy doing. You are more than what you look like.

In Your First Aid Kit

Things will go wrong with your health however careful you are, so make sure you have a well-stocked first aid kit available when you move out of home.

Contents of your first aid kit

- Products for the care of wounds or cuts — Alcohol cleansing pads and Neosporin cream are both good choices.
- Adhesive strips (e.g., Band-Aids)
- A painkiller such as acetaminophen (e.g., Tylenol)
- An anti-inflammatory such as ibuprofen (e.g., Advil) for headaches, period pain, or migraines
- Antihistamine pills (for hay fever or allergies)

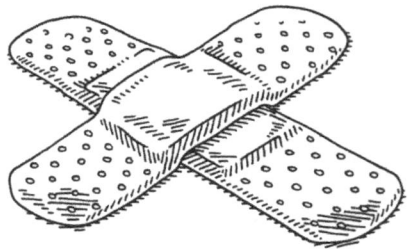

- A 1% steroid cream. This anti-itch cream is available at the drug store and is great to use when you have an insect bite or rash.

- A compression bandage (elastic bandage, ACE bandage) — for musculoskeletal injuries that require compression and support. Don't get this confused with one of those flimsy crepe bandages that are used to keep dressings on.

- Wound dressings of different sizes

- An eye bath (that little plastic oval cup on a tiny stem — like a squished egg cup)

- Condoms. Okay, maybe these aren't quite in the first aid box, but if you are sexually active or likely to be, have some stashed somewhere.

What Do I Do Now That I'm Sick?

Home Remedies

Yesterday you felt fine, but today something weird is going on. Your throat's feeling scratchy, or you have sprained your wrist, or you lost a tooth (hopefully not all at the same time). Here's what you need to do:

Coughs and colds

To avoid getting a cold, try to keep yourself healthy (see the drill above: eat well, exercise regularly, and also get enough sleep), wash your hands frequently with soap (those nasty cold germs are lurking everywhere), and avoid touching your eyes, nose, and mouth. If you do succumb, try the following:

- Get plenty of rest. Take time out from work or studying, and avoid spreading the misery to all your friends.

- Keep your fluids up — clear soup (even from a can) is good as is tea or warm water with lemon squeezed into it.

- Take a decongestant pill or use a nasal spray to clear your nose.

- Take a pain killer for headaches and a sore throat.

- Try gargling with salty warm water or dispersible aspirin (dissolved in water) every four hours (spit it out, don't swallow it). Dissolved aspirin has the added benefit of being an anti-inflammatory, directly hitting the spot where it's needed.

- Try inhalation by putting a towel over your head and breathing in the steam from a bowl of boiling water. Old fashioned but it works great. You can add a couple of drops of eucalyptus oil if you like.

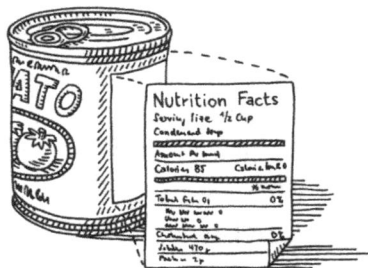

See a GP if you continue to have a fever or are not improving after 3–4 days.

Sprains and strains

If you have a sprain, remember RICE

If you injure yourself and have a sprain or strain, remember RICE:

Rest – Rest the injured part. Stop doing anything that aggravates it, which could include playing competitive sports, taking exercise classes, or running. Don't try to push through the pain, as you could increase the damage.

Ice – Apply any of the following for 15 minutes, followed by at least a 15-minute break:

- Ice or an ice pack wrapped in a dishtowel

- Ice and water in a Ziploc bag wrapped in a dishtowel

- A paper cup with water frozen in it and kept in the freezer for this purpose. Peel off the top part of the cup to expose the ice, hold on to the bottom part, and rub it on the site (an ice massage).

Continue this as required for up to 24 hours after the injury, after which time there will be little further benefit. Do not leave ice directly on the injured part as it is too cold and can cause injury to the skin.

Compression – Apply a compression bandage to help minimize swelling.

Elevation – Keep the injured part higher than the heart.

If required, take some pain-relieving medication such as acetaminophen (Tylenol). If severe pain continues or there is significant bruising or loss of function, seek medical advice.

Burns

- Remove the source of the burn from the patient or vice versa.

- Place the burn under cold running water, or immerse the affected part in a bucket of cold water for 20 minutes. Dressings designed for the safe and effective treatment of burns (such as Burnaid) are an excellent choice and are increasingly available, but don't confuse them with normal dressings. Never apply anything else, such as butter, aloe vera, ice packs, toothpaste (weird but some people do), or any sort of cream.

- See the doctor if the burn is very painful or involves the face, hands, genitals, or joints. Call an ambulance (yep, it's 911) if the burn involves the eyes or if it is larger in area than half your arm.

- Take a pain killer.

- After a few days, see a doctor if the burn shows any sign of infection. This could be increasing redness, pain, or the development of a sort of furry crust.

See the doctor if the burn is very painful

Cuts and bleeding

- Apply pressure with a clean pad (e.g., a dishtowel). If nothing is available, use your hand or someone else's hand.
- Elevate the affected part.
- Keep calm and still for at least the first 10 minutes.
- If blood soaks through the pad, don't take it off but apply another one on top.
- Seek medical care if you cannot control the bleeding or the cut is very deep.

Knocked-out tooth

If you lose a tooth, wash it in saliva and replace it into the mouth, trying not to touch the root of the tooth. You can use aluminum foil to keep it in place. If you can't replace it, store it in milk, sterile saline or saliva, or wrap it in Saran Wrap. You can also store it in your mouth, next to the cheek. Seek immediate dental advice as you have the greatest chance of saving the tooth if you can replant it within 15–20 minutes.

Menstrual pain

- Apply local heat (e.g., a hot water bottle or a heat pack).
- Take ibuprofen (Advil).
- Do some exercise (weird, but it can help).

If this is a persistent problem and interfering with your ability to carry out day-to-day activities, speak to your doctor, who may recommend taking the contraceptive pill.

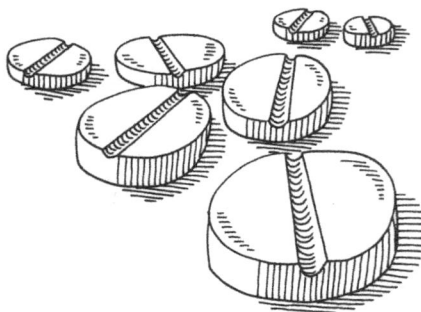

Hangovers

Okay, so you know that you are not legally allowed to drink before you turn 21. If you do decide to drink, hangovers are best avoided of course! Duh. Try to drink a glass of water before you start drinking (so you are not using the alcohol to quench your thirst), and then alternate soda or water with each glass of alcohol. If you do end up with a hangover, try these steps:

- Rehydrate. Drink lots of water, preferably before you go to bed.
- Take some Tylenol (not aspirin, as this can irritate the stomach further).
- Have food with sugar which can help if you have the shakes.
- Drink thin soup, for nutrients that won't upset your stomach further.
- DO NOT have a "hair of the dog" (i.e., avoid alcohol until you are completely recovered).

Going to See the Doctor

Choosing a doctor

Going to see a doctor can be daunting, particularly if you are embarrassed about what's brought you there. It's good to establish a relationship with your GP, and you might need to try a few till you find someone you feel comfortable with. Try the clinic on campus for a start, or ask your friends who they use. Another good option is to get a referral from your pediatrician to a primary care physician.

Most Common Health Issues for Young Adults

The most common reasons for young people to see a doctor include mental health issues, sexually transmitted infections, contraception and pap tests, coughs and colds, infections, and injuries. Here's how they'll normally be treated.

Mental health issues

According to the National Alliance on Mental Illness (NAMI),[14] approximately one in five adults in the U.S will have a mental illness in any given year. If you think you may be one of them, please don't suffer alone. These disorders are clearly very common; your GP will not think you are weird in any way, and they are also treatable by medication and other therapies.

One in five adults will have a mental illness in any year

When you decide that you need help, you have a couple of options. You can go to see your GP to discuss what's bothering you, or you may be able to find help nearby on campus. Most universities have counseling services, and these can often be subsidized, which is always good news! Some will even have their own websites. Also available on campus are Alcoholics Anonymous and Narcotics Anonymous groups, so do an Internet search or ask at the university health services.

If you're not yet up to seeing someone face to face, look at the following websites. They are all slightly different, but look around, and you'll find one that suits you and your needs. You can get online support and information, and treatment options will be explained.

- *NAMI* (mental health information and support)
- *National Eating Disorders Association (NEDA)* (for eating disorders)

- *Reachout, OK2talk, and teenlifeline* (for depression and anxiety)
- *Children & Adults with ADD (CHADD)* (for people living with ADHD)

If things are really getting you down, remember there is always emergency help at the end of the phone. The National Suicide Prevention Hotline is 1-800-273-8255.

Case Study:
Tackle Mental Health Issues Early

Christopher had been feeling flat for about a year, and his grades at school were beginning to suffer. He still went out with his friends but wasn't really enjoying himself and tended to drink too much to compensate. He found that he was sleeping a lot and also had the occasional thought about suicide. He felt that he didn't want to talk about it to his parents or friends, as it felt weird and he didn't want them to think he was crazy.

Finally, a friend realized what was going on and convinced him to talk to a counselor. After two months of sessions and also reading up on the NAMI website, he began to feel there was light at the end of the tunnel. In hindsight, he wished that he'd gotten help earlier.

Lesson: If you think you might have a mental health issue, take a deep breath and go to see someone about it. You'll be glad you did.

Sexually transmitted infections (STI's)

According to Centers for Disease Control and Prevention (CDC),[15] the United States has the highest rate of STIs in the industrialized world, and to top it off, 50% of all sexually transmitted infections are among 15- to 24-year-olds. These include gonorrhea, syphilis, HIV, and chlamydia.

Gonorrhea, syphilis, and HIV — See a doctor if you notice a genital discharge or rash, particularly after unprotected sex, or if someone you are in a sexual relationship with has been diagnosed with one of these diseases. Antibiotics are used to treat gonorrhea and syphilis; HIV is treated with antiviral drugs.

Chlamydia — 67% of chlamydia cases reported each year are in the age group 15- to 24-year-olds (again, according to CDC).[16] Chlamydia produces no symptoms in either males or females, but can cause infertility in females. If you are sexually active you should be tested every year; testing is simple and only involves a urine test. Treatment is also simple — two antibiotic pills for you and your partner if the test is positive. See the doctor if someone you are in a sexual relationship with is diagnosed with this disease.

Chlamydia produces no symptoms

Pap test

If you are female, over 21, and have ever been sexually active, you need to have a Pap test every three years as recommended by the American Cancer Society (ACS),[17] even if you have been immunized with the HPV vaccine. This can be done in a couple of minutes by your GP or Ob/Gyn or at a clinic like Planned Parenthood. Newer technology testing for the presence of the HPV virus itself rather than for cell changes may soon allow the gap between tests to be extended to five years.

Coughs and colds

Most colds are caused by viruses that do not respond to antibiotics, and the doctor will recommend rest, fluids, and drug store medications to ease the symptoms. Sometimes you may have a secondary infection, particularly if you are asthmatic, which may require antibiotics.

Sports injuries

If severe pain continues after an injury, there is a lot of bruising, and/or movement is severely restricted, seek medical advice. Your GP may refer you for an x-ray to rule out a broken bone or to a physical therapist, sports medicine specialist, or orthopedic surgeon for further treatment.

Infectious mononucleosis ("mono")

If you have had more than a week or two of fatigue and a sore throat, you should see your GP to rule out mono. This is diagnosed by a blood test, and treatment largely involves rest. Antibiotics can give you a rash if you have mono. The doctor can provide assistance if you need to ask for special consideration from work or study.

Appendicitis

Appendicitis is common, and symptoms include central abdominal pain radiating to the right, loss of appetite, nausea, and fever. Treatment involves removing the appendix by surgery.

Torsion of the testes

This can be an incredibly painful condition where one testis (testicle or "ball") twists inside the scrotum and cuts off its own blood supply. Apart from pain, the testis can also

Torsion of the testes is an incredibly painful condition

be swollen. This is a medical emergency so go to your doctor straight away if you have sharp testicular pain as torsion of the testes requires surgery. But don't worry - it's quite rare and only affects one in 4000 young men.[18]

Contraception

Talk to your GP, a pharmacist, or a contraception clinic. Two popular options are:

- Condoms. (These can be embarrassing to buy but are cheap, you don't need to see a doctor, and — this is a big point, so listen up! — they provide protection against sexually transmitted infections such as HIV as well as hepatitis B and chlamydia.)
- The contraceptive pill or patch. (These are easy to use and can help with other problems, such as painful periods, but you need to get a prescription, and they don't protect against STIs.)

Other forms of contraception:

- An IUD (Intra-uterine device) or IUS (Intra-uterine system)
- Implants (e.g., Implanon) or shots
- A diaphragm, cap, or female condom
- Natural family planning methods such as noticing changes in vaginal mucus, keeping a diary of when you may be ovulating, or taking your temperature
- Emergency contraception. If you've had unprotected sex, you can take the "morning after pill." You need to see a doctor to get this, and ideally it should be taken within 24 hours of unprotected sex. After this, its effectiveness drops off.

Ideally, work out which form of contraception you might consider using before you are in the position of needing to use it. Look at a reliable source for further information, such as the *Planned Parenthood* website.[19]

Plan your contraception ahead of time

If you are embarrassed to see your usual family doctor, remember that once you are an adult, as part of patient confidentiality, they will never reveal to anyone else (parents included) that you have been to see them about this matter. Alternatively, if you would prefer to be more anonymous, type *contraceptive clinic* into your Internet browser to find somewhere near you that can help.

Immunizations

In terms of immunizations, by the time you leave home, you are pretty well off the hook. However, there are a couple of things to think about. If you are sexually active, you should have a chlamydia test every year. It is a simple urine test, and it is easily treatable. (Okay, so it's not an immunization, but I wanted to remind you!)

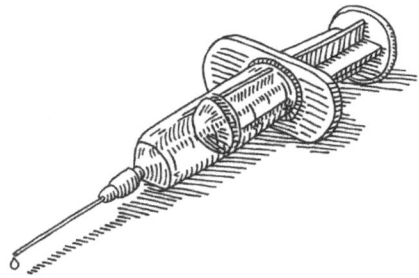

You should also have a tetanus booster every 10 years. You will have been immunized at the age of 11 to 12, so think about this when you turn 21.

Some of you may have had the HPV immunization when you were younger, but if not, talk to your doctor to see if this is appropriate for you now. HPV (or Human Papilloma Virus) is a very common infection that can lead to cancer of the cervix.

And finally, check with your doctor if you need a booster for chicken pox.

Dental Problems Affecting Young People

Cavities

Here's a weird but true fact: Leaving home can be bad for your teeth. There are a whole lot of reasons, including:

- Your diet going out the window, with you eating and drinking more sugary products.
- Your oral hygiene becoming less strict.
- Your level of socializing increasing so you are drinking more sugary and acidic alcohol and not drinking enough water.

All of this increases your risk of plaque, and you may end up with cavities, which can be very painful and not so attractive. See your dentist regularly for check-ups, and if you notice any problems in between times, take action sooner rather than later. This way you may avoid root and nerve problems and, eventually, lost teeth.

Leaving home can be bad for your teeth

Gum disease

When you clean your teeth, if what you spit out is pink, you may have gum disease (gingivitis). Although it is reasonably common, this is not normal and is usually the result of poor oral hygiene, so make sure you clean your teeth well (see later in this chapter) and go visit your friendly dentist regularly.

If untreated, gum disease can lead to periodontal disease and tooth loss. Also, in the longer term, the bugs causing gum disease can affect your ability to get pregnant or can result in a pre-term birth. They have also been linked to poor heart health.

Case Study:

Cavities

Taylor finished school last year and went to college. She was having a great time, going to lots of parties, sleeping in (and missing just that occasional lecture), and generally going wild. She noticed some bleeding when she was brushing her teeth and finally figured out that a trip to the dentist would be a good idea. She was shocked to discover she had three cavities that had to be filled which resulted in a huge dental bill. She wished someone had told her to look after her teeth when she moved out of home.

Lesson: Moving out can be dangerous for your teeth.

Eruption of wisdom teeth

One thing your dentist will keep an eye on at your regular visits will be your wisdom (3rd molar) teeth, which normally come through between the ages of 17 and 25. Sometimes they can cause grief when they are impacted (not descending properly and hitting other teeth nearby), or they can become partially descended and then infected. Often there is significant pain. Any of these reasons may indicate that they require removal, which can be done either in the dentist's chair with a local anesthetic or you may need a general anesthetic.

Sports and teeth

Sports are great for your general health but can be bad for your teeth! Apart from the risk of losing a tooth, you may end up drinking a lot of sports drinks, which are not recommended by dentists, as they are both very sweet and very acidic. If you really have to drink them, rinse your

Sports drinks are very sweet and acidic

mouth out with water as soon as you can. (But on the other hand, avoid dehydration as this can cause decay due to inadequate saliva to wash and neutralize the acid in your mouth.)

Mouth guards are important if you are playing a contact sport, and custom-made is best as they fit well. They are expensive but may be partly subsidized by your health insurance, and as an adult, your mouth doesn't change shape, so you can keep them for a number of years. That is, unless you put them through a hot wash, but even then they might survive! Ones from the drug store that you mold in hot water are better than nothing, but they may be uncomfortable and won't sit well over your teeth, meaning a lower level of protection and a risk of choking.

Other Dental Issues

Much of the following information is adapted from *The Young Person's Oral Survival Guide*, with thanks to the ADA.[20]

Tooth whitening

Be careful using tooth whitening kits — they may not be suitable for everyone, and the bleach in them can cause permanent side effects, such as burns, uneven tooth color, and increased oral sensitivity. See your dentist if you want whiter teeth.

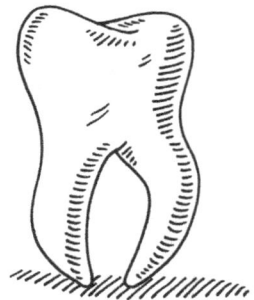

Orthodontic treatment

If you have always hated the shape of your teeth, you can still have braces as an adult. An orthodontist can advise you on the best option. Treatment time is different in each case but can take a number of years.

Binge Drinking

Binge drinking is not a great thing. It can cause you to make questionable decisions, it's bad for your health, and get this — it's even bad for your teeth! It not only exposes your teeth to the sugar and acid found in alcoholic drinks but it also increases the likelihood that you will forget to brush your teeth before you go to bed. Try to rinse your mouth out with water after every alcoholic drink, chew sugar-free gum, and brush your teeth before you go to bed. Leaving a toothbrush on your pillow can help to remind you about brushing.

Vomiting as a result of binge drinking floods your mouth with acid. If you are in any condition to do so, try to remember to brush your teeth or at least rinse out your mouth with water afterwards.

Smoking

There are three main mouth problems caused by smoking:

- Smoking can disguise tooth and gum damage. Damaged gums are normally red and they bleed easily when brushed, but damaged gums belonging to smokers do not. Smoking can therefore make it difficult for dentists to diagnose problems.
- The nicotine in smoke affects saliva production. Saliva helps prevent damage from acids, so this benefit may be diminished in smokers.
- Finally, smoking is the leading cause of oral cancer.

Smoking is the leading cause of oral cancer

If you can, stop smoking. If you can't, be careful with your brushing and flossing, and make sure you see your dentist regularly.

Piercings

Tongue and lip piercings can cause damage to your teeth and gums as well as nerve damage, which can cause numbness and speech problems. See your dentist if you are thinking about having this done so that you are aware of all the risks before you make your decision.

Illegal drugs

Illegal drugs can cause tooth grinding, a dry mouth, tooth decay, and gum disease. To help prevent this, maintain good oral hygiene, don't rub drugs onto your gums, chew sugar-free gum, cut back on sugary drinks and foods, and see your dentist regularly. Give them up if you can (see later in this chapter).

Dental Care

Here's how to keep your teeth sparkling till you are as old as your parents. Avoiding problems:

- Snack on savory foods rather than sweet ones.
- Drink lots of water, and make it tap rather than bottled, although if there is no other choice, bottled water is better than soda.
- Which brings us to: Avoid sugary drinks. Even sugar-free drinks contain a lot of tooth-eroding acid. If you can't avoid them, drink them through a straw, and swish your mouth with water after you've finished them.
- Chew sugar-free gum. It's better for your diet than sugary gum but is also good for

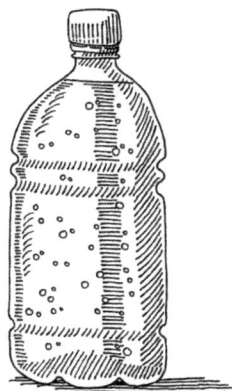

your teeth because it increases protective saliva production, and the chewing itself may decrease the risk of cavities.

- See the dentist as frequently as every six months to a year — maybe more if you are a smoker or diabetic, maybe less if you are a good flosser. Going to the dentist can be expensive unless you have dental insurance (either in your own plan or under your parents'), in which case you will have part if not all of the cost rebated. So you don't forget, schedule in dentist appointments in between semesters.

Checklist: Brushing your teeth

Make sure you are doing the following:

✔ Brushing your teeth twice a day for two minutes with a fluoride toothpaste and a soft toothbrush.

✔ Using a soft toothbrush, massaging the gums, and brushing the teeth with small circular motions.

✔ Avoiding scrubbing horizontally and making sure you brush all surfaces of the teeth, including the inside.

✔ Flossing to remove plaque and food debris every day (yes, really); leaving your dental floss in the shower can be a good reminder.

✔ Throwing away your toothbrush when it is looking shaggy, at least every three months.

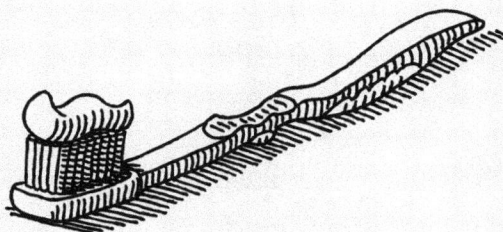

Issues Relating to the Party Life

Socializing may or may not form a big part of your life, but it's worthwhile remembering a few things to keep you and your friends safe when you go out.

Checklist: How to party safely

Make sure you follow these tips:

✔ Plan at the start of the night how you will get home, not at the end.

✔ If you plan to be drinking, eat a full meal before you go out (including protein, such as meat, cheese, eggs, or dairy) — it slows the absorption of the alcohol.

✔ Stay with your friends, and look out for each other.

✔ Trust your own judgment — if it seems dicey, it probably is.

✔ Stay in a safe environment — streets with enough lighting that aren't too quiet. And if it looks like things are getting out of control or a fight is brewing, leave and go somewhere else.

✔ Remember that you can have a great time without trashing yourself. Drink water or soda in between alcoholic drinks, and try not to drink in a round or drinking game as you can end up drinking more than you want.

✔ Don't drink and take drugs at the same time.

✔ Know how much you are drinking — pour your own drinks, and don't let others top you up.

✔ Don't leave your drink lying around – it can be a target for spikers and result in sexual assault.

✔ Don't experiment with new drugs while you're out – if it's something you really feel you have to do, make sure you are somewhere safe and with friends. Also remember that it's dangerous to use by yourself.

✔ Don't drink and drive or let your friends do it.

✔ Don't swim if you're drunk or have taken drugs.

✔ Don't have unprotected sex – carry condoms.

✔ Don't walk home alone – have the number of someone you can call even if it's really late.

How to look after a drunk friend

Drug and Alcohol Research and Training Australia (DARTA) provides this information, with thanks to Paul Dillon.[21]

You know that getting drunk can cause all sorts of problems to your health and to your security. But a hangover isn't the worst part – alcohol poisoning can also kill you. This happens in three ways: It can suppress your heart and breathing to the point where you stop breathing and your heart stops beating, you can become unconscious and choke on your own vomit, or it can react with other drugs or medications you have taken.

So if you are in the position of looking after a drunk friend, please do the following:

- Stick with them, and never leave them alone – not even to go to the bathroom. They could lock the door and become unconscious with you unable to get in.

You can have a great time without trashing yourself

- Monitor them. The line between being drunk and being poisoned can be fine, and if a person is already unwell and has drunk alcohol in the past hour or so, it could still be in the process of being absorbed, and they will get worse. Stay there until they are feeling better.

Never leave a drunk friend alone

- Reassure them. When you are unwell after drinking, it can be very frightening. It's important to have friends nearby.

- Keep them comfortable. If they are feeling sick, they may feel feverish, so putting a cold compress (or even a cold water bottle) on the back of the person's neck can make them feel much more comfortable. Make sure that there is also something warm to wrap around them just in case they start to get cold.

- Keep them hydrated. This can be difficult. If they are not getting sick, make sure they replace lost fluids (i.e., if they have been urinating a lot, they need to drink water). For someone who is vomiting, soak a T-shirt or cloth in cold water and then have the person suck on that in between being sick. That way they are rehydrating and also making their mouth feel a little more pleasant but not gulping down water that is likely to make them vomit more.

- If in doubt, call for help. It is not an issue if, by the time the ambulance arrives, everything is okay. Also, it's important to know that the police will not attend a medical emergency involving alcohol or other drugs unless another crime, such as violence, has taken place.

Checklist: When to call an ambulance

How do you know if a person is just drunk or is suffering from alcohol poisoning? Seek emergency medical help if:

✔ The person is unconscious and can't be woken up by pinching, prodding, or shouting.

✔ The skin is cold, clammy, pale, or bluish or purplish in color, indicating that they're not getting enough oxygen.

✔ The person is breathing very slowly. If there are more than 10 seconds between breaths, this is an emergency.

✔ The person is vomiting without waking up.

Ambulance costs

A mix of different organizations provides ambulance services, and you may or may not be able to get a free ride depending on where you live. Private insurance generally covers ambulance trips of an emergency nature, which is just as well as these can be very expensive (up to $2,000 for one trip).

But I'd like to make one point here – remember, whatever your insurance, if you need an ambulance, call one. If you are worried that the police will be involved, remember that they are only concerned if a crime has taken place. Paramedics are just interested in keeping you alive.

Drugs

We're talking about illegal drugs here. If you do choose to use drugs, remember:

- Don't ever be coerced into drug taking. It's your body, and you have the right to decide what goes into it.
- Make sure that you don't use alone and that there is a non-drug-taking friend to look after you. Tell them what you are going to take, and tell them if you don't feel well.
- Don't swim; keep away from water or other potentially risky situations; don't use and drive.
- Don't mix your drugs (and that includes taking alcohol and drugs together).
- Remember that drugs affect people differently, so what might have suited your friend might not be good for you.

Don't ever be coerced into drug taking

- While you can never be sure, try to know what it is you are taking.
- Don't use drugs by injection — it creates a whole different set of issues to consider.
- Use a condom if you are having sex. Every time.
- Don't ever be involved with drugs overseas. Other countries have different laws than ours, and many have the death penalty for drug-related crimes.

Where can I get help with a drug or alcohol problem?

If you need help for yourself, a friend, or a family member who has an alcohol or other drug problem, go to the following:

- If it's information you're after, go to the National Institute on Drug Abuse at www.drugabuse.gov. You'll find lots of fact sheets, articles, and web pages about different drugs as well as how to get help or referrals.
- If it's help you need but you would rather just call first, try 1-800-662-HELP, which can refer you for treatment at nearby facilities.

Five Top Tips

1. If someone at home or at work is sick, wash your hands frequently. It can stop you from catching whatever they've got.

2. Place a burn in cold water for 20 minutes, and avoid using anything else, such as Aloe Vera, butter, or ice packs.

3. Replace a knocked-out tooth into your mouth after washing with milk or saliva, and see a dentist within 15–20 minutes. This gives you the best chance of saving it.

4. If you are looking after a drunk friend, stick with them, and don't leave them alone — not even for them to go to the toilet.

5. If you think you might need an ambulance, just call one. Don't be concerned about the cost, whether one is really necessary, or whether the police will become involved. Police are only concerned if a crime has taken place, whereas paramedics just want to keep you alive.

CHAPTER 7

Clothing Care 101

Y ou know how at home the dirty clothes in the hamper just appear back in your closet and are sometimes even ironed? Sadly, that magic stops when you move out. If you don't take action yourself, you'll end up looking like your little brother on a bad day. Or worse.

Haven't Got Time to Read the Whole Chapter? Read This.

1. There is a care tag on all of your clothes that will tell you whether they can be machine-washed, what temperature you should use, and how you should dry them. Read this to avoid washing disasters.

2. Want to avoid ironing? Always remove clothes immediately from the dryer once they are dry. Put them away carefully as well and your iron may never see the light of day.

3. Shoes need care, so clean them, polish them, and have them re-soled or re-heeled as required. That way they'll last longer and look better.

4. Different types of jewelry require different types of care. Gold should be soaked in warm water, silver should be cleaned with silver cleaner or using baking soda and aluminum foil, pearls should be washed or wiped, and diamonds are best done in a jewelry store.

5. Moths love stains on natural fabrics, so make sure your woolens are put away clean. At the first sign of a moth or larvae, take action. Protect your clothes by washing them, and then get serious with the moths.

What do you need?

You'll need something to collect and carry your dirty clothes in (a hamper, a basket, a big old shopping bag) and some suitable laundry detergent. Choose one for cold water and you've got most cases covered, and make sure it is suited to the type of machine that is available — either front-loader for a machine with a door at the front (the detergent for these will say "HE" on the bottle) or top-loader for a lid at — you guessed it! — the top. You'll also need soap for woolens or delicates to use when you are washing by hand.

And don't forget a supply of coins if you have a dryer available in your building and it's a pay-as-you-go type of machine. Many dorms have pre-paid cards for their machines.

Timing Your Washing

Unless you have your own machine in your apartment, you'll probably find that when you want to do your washing, there will also be a line of other people with the same idea, so it can be a good idea to wash at odd times. Don't try on the weekend — that's when every man and his dog are also trying to get their clothes clean. How about you try on Tuesday mid-morning? Or before you go to bed on Wednesday night? Or even get up earlier and put your washing in before lectures? (Okay, agreed. Maybe getting up early to do your washing IS a little drastic.) Just don't try to do it Saturday afternoon or Sunday at lunchtime.

How to Wash Your Clothes

There are four main ways of washing your clothes — in the machine, by hand, soaking (actually, I'm not sure this counts as washing), and dry cleaning. Don't dry clean your everyday clothes. Apart from the inconvenience of driving to the dry cleaner's, who knows what chemicals they use? Do you really want to put them against your skin? You've got to be kidding. And not only that but it's really expensive. Of course, you may have to dry clean precious items such as winter coats, suits, or evening wear, but don't make it a habit for your run-of-the-mill items.

Machine washing

Before you wash anything, always make sure you read the care tag (which is different to the size or brand tag) on the inside of your clothes. You'll find that most items can be machine washed, especially jeans, shorts, t-shirts, hoodies, pajamas, underwear, and sports gear (but not specialized compression wear if you want it to last).

Materials that are NOT good candidates for going in the washer include silk, some wools, special finish items (e.g., anti-mosquito clothing), formal wear, and clothes with a decorative finish (such as sequins).

Machine washing top tips

- Wash your colored clothes and your whites separately to avoid graying the whites. The one exception to this is that you can wash light blue clothes with the whites. In fact, in the olden days, people used to add a "bluing agent" to their whites — which bizarrely made them seem whiter. Be particularly careful not to wash anything red with your whites or you'll end up pink all over. Also be particularly diligent on the first few washes of new items, when colors are most likely to run.

- Use hot water for whites and cold or warm water for colors. This will help keep your colors brighter for longer.

- Wash black items inside out (to maintain their "blackness"), and avoid using detergents with optical whiteners as they cause black clothes to fade. Look at the side of the detergent box.

- Spray stain remover on cuffs and collars of shirts that are grubby before you add them to the machine. Wait a minute before you turn the machine on to allow the stain remover to act.

- Use the right detergent for your machine (i.e., for a top-loader or a front-loader) and for the temperature of water you have chosen.

- Look at the box to see how much detergent the manufacturer recommends. Halve it, and you'll find that the clothes will generally still come out clean.

Wash black items inside out to avoid fading

- Make sure you add detergent before you add the clothes as this helps it dissolve, which means you don't get powdery marks on your clothes.

- If an item is stained, wash the stain as soon as possible. A soak in COLD water is a good thing. Hot water can make some stains permanent.

- Use a net washing bag for items that you want to protect from rubbing (such as small delicate items) or from stretching (such as tights). Also, place underwire bras into a bag as a loose underwire in the washing machine's workings can lead to an expensive repair fee.

Hand washing

You'll need to hand wash some items, particularly ones that are made of wool or silk or are very delicate. Also, some sportswear should be hand washed, and if so, it will say so on the tag. Personally, I find hand washing a real bore, but it can't be helped. Here's an effective way to do it:

- Dissolve hand washing liquid, simple soap, or shampoo (but definitely not detergent) in warm water. Make sure the water isn't hot.

- Immerse the clothes, and gently swish around – no stretching, pulling, or wringing.

- Leave to soak for about five minutes.

- Pull the plug out, and drain. Rinse by refilling the sink with warm water and gently swishing the item around; pull the plug out, and drain again. Gently squeeze the excess moisture out.

- Lay the item on a towel on the floor, and then roll up the towel.

- Stand on it (yes, stand on it), stepping along the length of the towel. This dirties your towel but gets most of the water out of your precious item, which helps avoid any of the dangers associated with hanging the item up (in particular, stretching). If it's not too precious, you can spin dry in the machine on a gentle setting instead.

- Hang, well supported, on a drying rack. Be careful if hanging outside as the sun can cause delicate items to fade. Woolens are best laid flat to dry to avoid stretching.

Soaking

Soaking is your friend when you are in a time crunch and active (read: dirty). Camping gear and winter sports gear just love a good soak. Just fill your sink with warm water, add detergent (powder or liquid), agitate the water to make sure it dissolves, and toss the items in. If they are (were) white, you can use a soaker designed for the purpose, such as a bleaching solution.

Avoid soaking different colors together

Avoid soaking different colors together as the color may leach or soaking items with metal trims, which may leave rust stains if soaked for longer than an hour. Also make sure that you soak all of the item, not just the affected part, as you can end up with color changes in the soaked area that will look rather strange once dry.

Soak from an hour to several days, and then machine wash as usual.

Stain Removal

- In general, the quicker you get to a stain, the more successful you will be with its removal.

- If there is some solid matter to the stain (e.g., food, mud, blood), remove the excess with a blunt knife, and then treat.

- If in doubt, rinse in cold water until as much of the stain is removed as possible, and then soak. If the stain is of a greasy nature, use warm water.

There are a few types of stains that require special treatment.

STAIN	TREATMENT
Chewing gum	Freeze, and then scrape off any excess and dab with eucalyptus oil. Wash.
Ink	Be careful! Refer to a dry cleaner as soon as possible. Do not wash as this may spread and/or set the stain, but if you are desperate, sponge with rubbing alcohol.
Lipstick	Dab with rubbing alcohol.
Mud & paint	Use <u>hot</u> water to clean. If the stain remains after washing, use a commercial stain remover.
Sunscreen	Dab with rubbing alcohol; then wash.
Wine	Pour on seltzer water; then soak as usual.

Drying

Only tumble dry things you are sure can stand it — jeans, casual clothes, underwear, pajamas, and most sports gear. Some socks and t-shirts don't like it, so if in doubt, hang them up to dry. Never wool! Never silk! Never the cat!

If you don't want to burn your house down, clean out the lint from the dryer every now and then (like every time actually).

And if you ever get the chance to string a line and hang out your washing, do it! Line drying your clothes means they smell fresh, they won't wear out so quickly and it's better for the environment. If they're white, the sun will help keep them that way. Good news all round. With hanging out, the general rule is that you hang tops from the bottom (e.g., a t-shirt gets hung from its bottom hem) and bottoms from the top (e.g., a pair of jeans gets hung from the waistband).

Ironing

If you can possibly find a roommate who likes ironing, then grab them with two hands and never let them go (but not in a weird way). Some people like ironing in front of TV, although if you're like me, nothing can make ironing a pleasure. So it's important to know how to do it properly to minimize the time required. Follow the steps below to make it easy. Well, easier.

Avoid ironing if you can

When you are clothes shopping, look for items that won't need ironing. Yay! Remove items promptly from the dryer — hot, scrunched up clothes will lead to cold, really scrunched up clothes! Don't leave them jumbled in the laundry basket. And finally, if you are taking a shower, try hanging the item you need to press in the bathroom with you and leave the fan off – the steam can make creases disappear.

Buy clothes that won't need ironing

Preheat the iron

Always check that you have the iron on the correct temperature for the item of clothing you are ironing. Yes! There are different settings on an iron ranging from synthetic (very cool) to linen (very hot). If you don't use the right setting for the right item of clothing, you could end up with a disaster, such as melting a synthetic top if the iron is too hot or wasting your time and achieving nothing on linen if the iron is too cool.

Fill the iron with water, and have it set on "steam" if you are ironing very creased items of clothing or those made from cotton or linen. Similarly, it can help to have a spray bottle of water handy to dampen the item before you run the iron over it. Makes ironing a breeze.

If possible, have a very large ironing board. Ironing boards are amazingly expensive, and you may think it's a waste of money buying a large one when you plan not to be doing too much ironing at all! If you have the budget and the storage space, buy a big one as it will minimize time spent ironing, which has to be a good thing

One last tip: If you tumble dry a dry item with a damp towel, it can minimize the ironing required. Excellent.

Dress shirts

Here is one way to iron your dress shirts:

- Iron the collar, laying it out flat on the ironing board
- Now iron the outside (right side) of one cuff, unfolding it to do so, followed by the same sleeve, laying it flat on the ironing board to do so. Now do the other cuff and sleeve

- Iron one front yoke (the top of the front), then the back yoke, then the other front yoke.

- Finally, iron the back then the two fronts. This means you iron the part you are most likely to see last so it does not run the risk of being crushed while you iron the rest of the shirt.

Pants

Ironing pants can be tricky. The key here is to iron them laying them down on their side so that you end up with a crease down the front and the back of each pant leg. Lay them on the ironing board sideways, iron the inside of one leg and the outside of the other then flip them over and iron the inside of the other leg and the outside of the other. All done.

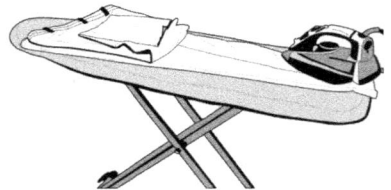

T-shirts

Okay, these are easy — just lay them flat with the front facing you and iron the sleeves first, followed by the body. If you are fussy or the fabric is thick, turn them over and iron the sleeves and body of the other side. But remember that t-shirts tend to look less creased as you wear them, so some people never iron t-shirts at all.

You've got to be kidding

Never, ever bother to iron the following: jeans, sheets, dishtowels or underwear (need I say more?).

Shoe & Jewelry Care

Leather shoes

If you splash out for a really expensive pair of work shoes or fabulous boots, you want them to last, and one way to achieve that is to polish them regularly.

Again, there's no absolutely right way to do it, but here's one method:

- Clean off any mud with a coarse brush that you keep for this purpose.
- Apply shoe polish smoothly with another coarse brush. Make sure it's not too thick but that you take particular care of the toes and heels (where a lot of scuffing occurs).
- Leave for a couple of minutes; then brush off with a softer polishing brush
- Finally, buff with a soft cloth.

Stuff wet shoes with newspaper

If your shoes are wet, stuff them with newspaper, and allow them to dry away from heat before you clean them. This will prevent the leather from cracking.

For really good shoes, keep an eye on the soles and, in particular, the heels. A shoe repairer can replace both soles and heels so that you get another few years of life out of your precious shoes. It can be expensive but worth it if you really like them.

Patent leather shoes

Clean with Vaseline (petroleum jelly) — yes, really!

Suede shoes

Don't get suede shoes wet — this will mark them irreversibly. Never use any sort of polish on them but instead brush them with a special suede brush bought from a shoe store, or gently use steel wool. Suede shoes are not easy to clean, so be careful with them and try not to wear them on a wet day. Alternatively, to prevent stains, you can buy a waterproofing spray for suede shoes, although some people think this changes the breathability of the suede and you can end up with a stinky shoe. Or two.

Muddy sports and hiking boots

With sports boots (such as those for football, field hockey, lacrosse, etc.) or hiking boots, make sure you let them dry away from direct heat (never on a heater) as this can make the leather crack. Once dry, brush off the dried mud with a stiff brush. If they are still very dirty, use warm soapy water and a brush to clean them but try not to immerse them in the water. Then wipe them with a damp cloth and leave to dry.

Sports shoes

Most sneakers or sports shoes can be washed in warm soapy water, rinsed in clear warm water, and then left with the tongues pulled open to dry. Let them dry in the air outside, or hang them on the towel bar by their laces.

Cleaning Jewelry

Gold

To clean gold jewelry, soak it for 15 minutes in warm water with a splash of dishwashing liquid. Rinse with clear water. Because gold is a soft metal, be sure to store it away from other jewelry so that it doesn't get scratched.

Silver

Cleaning silver jewelry (and other silver items too) is an alchemist's dream! Silver cleaner works very well, but why don't you try this? Bring a large non-stick or stainless steel pot of water to a boil. Add in several tablespoons of baking soda and a large piece of scrunched up aluminum foil. Immerse your silver items in the frothing mess, and swirl around with a wooden spoon. Once they are clean (and this may take some more baking soda), rinse them with warm fresh water and leave them to dry on a dishtowel. Don't use an aluminum saucepan as you can end up with a black pan!

Pearls

Pearls are very delicate — they can scratch easily, and because they are porous, they are vulnerable to hairspray and perfume. Wash them in warm water with dishwashing liquid added, rinse them, and then let them dry on a soft towel. Try not to get them too wet as this can cause their thread to weaken and break. Store them in a soft pouch, and wear them often so that the oils in your skin improve their luster. Apparently pearls don't like sweat, so if you've been wearing your pearls to do a spin class, wipe them off before you put them away.

Diamonds and other stones

The best way to clean diamonds is by going to a jewelry store and asking if they would please clean them in their ultrasonic cleaner. (This works best if they know you or if you've actually bought something from the store.) Otherwise, at home, you can use warm water and detergent and a soft brush, but be careful as you don't want to damage the setting. You can also use a dental irrigation device to remove dirt from the claws.

Clothes Maintenance

You'll need a few things in your sewing kit to do any quick repairs or to take up a hem every now and then.

Checklist: Your sewing kit

Make sure you have the following:

✔ A collection of sewing needles, including different sized "sharps" (medium length with a sharp point and good for repair work) as well as a couple of different sized darning needles (bigger but not too sharp)

✔ A seam ripper for quickly unpicking stitching

✔ Good quality thread in black, white, and gray to start with. Work up to a whole rainbow of colors over time.

✔ Some embroidery scissors (about four inches long and small and sharp)

✔ A good pair of large fabric scissors. If you can, choose ones with an offset handle as they are the easiest to use.

✔ Something you can use to remove lint and fuzz from your clothes, either a shaver or a fabric comb

✔ A box of pins. The long ones with colored balls on the end are easy to use, and because of their color, you don't miss them when you are removing them.

✔ A tape measure

✔ A little box for collecting buttons as they come your way

✔ Some safety pins

Sewing on a button

Buttons are always coming off shirts, usually just as you are running out the door to a very important interview or a big night out! You can't always be heading back home to mom to get a button sewn on, and they only take a minute to do yourself, so it's a really useful skill to learn.

Sewing on a button is a useful skill

First of all, thread a sharp needle with a thread that is the length of about one and a half times the distance from your elbow to the tip of your finger. Pull the thread through the hole till one side is about twice the length of the other. Tie a knot in the end of the long side, and hold the button onto the fabric with your finger on one side and your thumb on the other where you want it to be located.

Starting on the inside of the item, come up through the fabric and then through one of the holes of the button that you are holding in place. Pull the thread all the way through. Place a pin horizontally across the button and go down into the other hole, over the top of the pin, and pull the thread all the way through. The reason you have a pin there is to give some slack to the thread as you are sewing on the button.

Then come up through the first hole again (or in the case of a four button hole, through the first of the other two holes) and down through the second (or fourth), repeating this about six times. Once you have done this, remove the pin on the top of the button, insert the needle from the

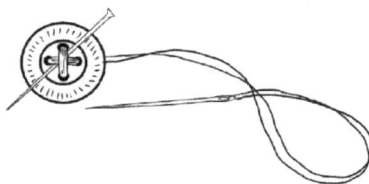

Using a pin to sew on a button

top to below the button but not through the fabric (so the needle is now between the button and the item of clothing) and wrap the thread around the shank a couple of times. Then pass the needle back down through the fabric to the inside of the garment, tie a knot, then cut it off. Easy!

Pilling or Fuzz

Pilling is when those little balls of fuzz suddenly appear on your sweater, particularly on woolen clothes, and in areas of wear, such as along your sleeves or under your arms. The best way to remove this is by using a little battery-operated clothing shaver designed for the purpose, but beware! You can put a hole in a cashmere sweater by over-enthusiastic shaving.

It's difficult to look smart with fuzzy clothes, so remove fuzz when you see it.

Mending

Repairing a small tear

Remember that old saying "A stitch in time saves nine"? You know that means you should fix something early on before it has time to develop into a big problem. (And if it does, see *Repairing a Large Hole Using a Patch*, later on in this chapter.)

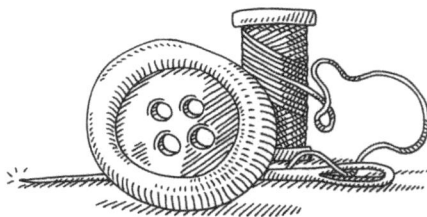

Try to get to the hole before it's much larger than ¼ of an inch. Thread a sharp needle with a matching color and type of thread. For instance, if it's a cotton item of clothing, use normal cotton thread. Over time, try to collect a set of good quality threads from a specialized sewing store, and don't use generic brand thread — it frays and breaks and can drive you crazy, not to mention leave you with another hole to fix. If the item is woolen, use a thicker woolen thread designed for mending purposes. You can also buy this at a sewing store.

A hole on a seam

If the hole is on a seam, you are in luck! Turn the clothing inside out and sew along the seam line, doing backstitch. (This is a very easy yet sturdy stitch — look at YouTube, and in two minutes you'll be backstitching like the best of them.) Or if that's not possible, just sew over the edge, enclosing the seam with each stitch (this is called overstitch). When you turn the clothing right side out again, you won't be able to see it. Easy.

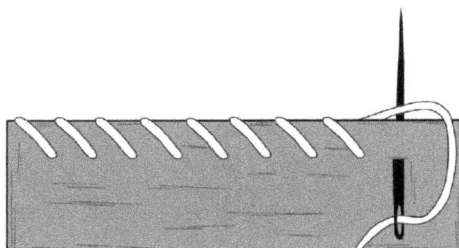

Overstitching a tear

A hole in the middle of the fabric

If it's not at a seam (i.e., it's in the middle of the fabric), lay the fabric flat or, even better, stretch it very slightly over a light bulb or a wooden darning mushroom.

Bring the needle up from underneath at the edge of the hole; then take the thread down through the middle of the hole and up through the edge of the fabric on the

A darning mushroom

opposite side of the hole. Then go down through the hole again and come up through the fabric next to where you took your first stitch. If you pull tightly on each stitch, you'll end up with something that looks like a spider joining it all together. Take the thread through to the underside, tie a knot, and cut it off.

Repairing a large hole using a patch

If it's a large hole, you can't just pull it together with stitching, as this will cause it to pucker. You will need to patch it. Cut a piece of fabric in a neat shape ½ inch larger all around than the hole, any shape you like but most commonly this is a square or a circle. Place it in the required place so that the hole is completely covered. Pin around the edges of the patch, making sure that you pin only the patch and the top layer together and not the back of the garment as well.

Beg, borrow, or steal a sewing machine, and sew as neatly as you can in a zigzag stitch around the edge of the patch. This can be tricky if it's on the leg of jeans, so you will have to slide the jeans on the arm of the machine and sew two sides, then take the jeans off, slide them on the other way, and sew the next two sides.

If you really can't get a machine, then using double thread, or even better, embroidery thread, sew around the patch with diagonal stitches in one direction and when you get to the start again, sew back around the other way, crossing each of the stitches. Take the thread down to the wrong side, tie a knot, and cut off the excess thread.

Darning

Darning is a skill that is fast disappearing. I'm not sure that anyone expects you to darn your socks, but trust me, it is very Zen, and there is a strange satisfaction in darning, so here goes: Put the sock on a light bulb or a darning mushroom, and thread a darning needle with matching woolen thread. Sew some long stitches across the hole in parallel lines. Then turn the socks 90°, and going above and below each of the parallel lines, do another row of parallel lines at right angles to the first set. It's like weaving. Once you have covered the hole, weave the end of the woolen thread through a part of undamaged sock for about one inch and then cut off the excess thread.

Darning is very Zen

Darning a hole in a sock

Taking Up Hems

Taking up pants or a skirt by hand

If you are trying to save money, a good place to start is by doing your own clothing alterations, and in particular, hems. It's not too difficult and in the time taken to drop off and pick up the item elsewhere, you could do it yourself. Go on! Have a go!

Try on your pants or skirt, and ask a friend to pin up a small part of the hem at approximately the right level. Look in the mirror, and check that it's the right length. When you are happy with the length of the hem, remove your item of clothing. If it's a skirt, slide it inside out on an ironing board; if it's a pair of jeans, lay them flat, inside out, on a table. Measure the amount of hem you need to fold up. A hand-sewn hem is usually larger than a machine sewn one – you will need about 1½ inches for the hem itself, so if, for instance, you need to fold up 5 inches, you will need to cut off 3½ inches. Very accurately cut off the required amount using a tape measure or ruler to guide you.

Using the iron, press ½ inch of the hem under onto the wrong side. Next fold over another 1 inch and press again (giving you the total of 1½ inches), and put pins through all layers at the top folded edge of the hem.

Thread a sharp needle with a matching colored thread, and tie a knot in the end of the thread. Insert the needle into the fold of the hem – travel ½ inch towards yourself; then bring the needle out of the hem fold. Now take a small stitch of the fabric and insert the needle back into the fold of the hem. Insert the needle again into the fold of the hem, pass it another ½ inch towards you, bring it out of the fold of the hem, then take another small stitch of the fabric, as in the diagram below.

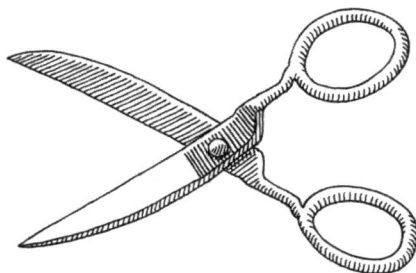

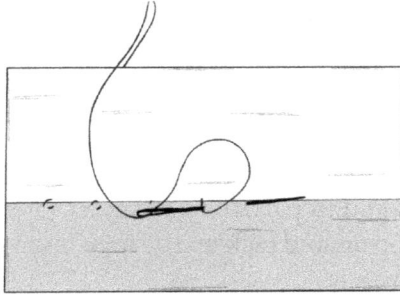

Hemming - inside of garment

Continue in this manner until you have gone around the whole hem. The end result is a hem that is reasonably secure where you can only see tiny stitches on the outside of the garment (as below). Tie the thread off securely.

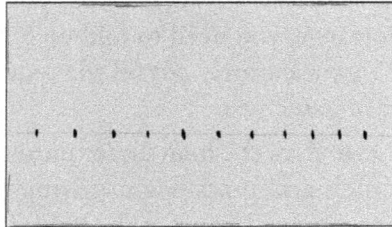

Hemming - outside of garment

Taking up pants or a skirt by machine

This is very similar to taking up pants or a skirt by hand, but as machine hems are narrower than hand-sewn hems, you will need only one inch for the hem itself. So if the fold up you have is 5 inches, you will need to cut off 4 inches all around. Very accurately cut off the required amount using a tape measure or ruler.

Using the iron, press ⅓ inch of the hem up onto the wrong side. Now press up the next ⅔ inch and pin through all layers of fabric at the top folded edge of the hem.

Using a sewing machine and a straight stitch of medium length, sew through the hem all the way around on the inside. When you get to the start of the stitching again, take a few more stitches, and then reverse for a few stitches. The end result will be a very strongly stitched hem with the stitches visible from the outside. This is an ideal hem to use for jeans.

Storing Your Clothes

Folding versus hanging

Always fold your sweaters rather than hanging them to avoid the stretching caused by coat hangers. The opposite is true for dress shirts; it is better to hang them to avoid the creases caused by folding them.

Always fold your sweaters to avoid stretching them

Shoe storage

Shoes can be smelly, and ones that you use regularly are much better left on a shoe rack to air than hidden away in a drawer. Good shoes, though, are best left in a shoebox as they are protected from rubbing against other shoes.

One thing to remember is that it's good to avoid wearing shoes two days in a row as they need to dry off between wears. This can be difficult to achieve, but it's better for your shoes if you can.

And Finally...Moths

Types of moths

Did you know there are two types of household moths? The first ones are those horrible ones that seem to appear from nowhere in your pantry – Indian meal moth or Plodia interpunctella (such a great name!)

to be exact.[22] The second ones are the ones that enjoy eating the favorite and generally most expensive items in your closet. Clothing moths (or Tineola bisselliella, if you need to know) love natural fabrics, in particular wool and cashmere, and even better if they have had human sweat, food, or liquids dropped on them.

The eggs and larvae are tiny and very difficult to see. Often the first evidence of a moth invasion is when you find the white fluffy cocoons they leave behind. That is, until you hold up your favorite item and it is littered with holes and looks like lace. What a disaster!

How do you get rid of larvae and eggs?

Moths are not interested in clothes that are washed regularly or in frequent use. But if you are going to put away clothes for a couple of months, make sure they are very clean.

You can do any of the following to kill the eggs and larvae:

- Wash them in water that is 140° or hotter (but be careful with your wools as they can shrink)
- Put your clothes in a plastic bag in the freezer for several days
- Put them in a plastic bag in the hot sun for several hours
- Dry clean your clothes

It is unlikely that moths will be hanging out in any synthetic clothes or any of your sturdier work or weekend wear, so concentrate on the natural fibers in your closet.

How do you get rid of adult moths?

So, clean your clothes, and once you have the larvae under control, you can now attack the adult moths so they are no longer able to breed. The best way is to use hormone traps — they have a pheromone lure that attracts the male moth. Once all the male moths are stuck to the sticky trap, the poor females die from broken hearts, and there are no more baby moths. Cool. These traps are available at most grocery stores.

You may also need to use a Pyrethroid surface spray on all surfaces of your closet. Do not spray this directly on to your clothes. These chemicals can be toxic to cats and fish and are not great for humans either, so use them in moderation.

Finally, when you are not wearing your woolens for some time, make sure they are clean, and then store them in their own plastic bags in your closet.

What shouldn't you use?

Old-fashioned mothballs made of naphthalene are toxic if ingested by children or pets, they produce a gas that is carcinogenic, and they are flammable. There is nothing good to say about mothballs (apart from the fact that they can come in pretty colors), and they should be avoided.

Camphor wood chests have been used for centuries to help keep moth infestations at bay, but although they smell great, it is doubtful whether the camphor-wood vapor builds up to the point where it can kill the larvae. The value of these chests lies more in the fact that they are well sealed and the moths can't access the clothes.[23]

So that's it for looking after your clothes. Good luck!

Don't use mothballs. They are toxic and flammable, and produce a gas which is carcinogenic

Five Top Tips

1. Don't machine wash silk, most wools, formal wear, and clothes with a decorative finish.

2. The quicker you get to a stain, the easier it is to remove it. Always choose cold water for soaking unless it's mud or paint, in which case use warm.

3. To keep the dryer working effectively, clean out the lint every time you use it. This will also avoid it catching on fire!

4. Make sure you set your iron to the right temperature for the type of fabric you are ironing. For instance, linen needs a hot iron; synthetics need a cool one.

5. Clean patent leather shoes with Vaseline and suede shoes with steel wool.

CHAPTER 8

My House Is A Pigsty

I f you are living in a dorm, you can skip this chapter. Just remember to clean your room every now and then. Time it for when your parents are visiting and everyone's happy.

But if you are living in an apartment, have you got a roommate who loves cleaning? A friend who wants to tidy up your new apartment? Or a genie in a bottle? Darn. It's going to be up to you then.

Haven't Got Time to Read the Whole Chapter? Read This.

1. Do some cleaning every day (just a small amount) and a bigger clean every week. Don't leave it till your place is filthy or till someone special is coming to visit as by then it will be a task suited only to the Fantastic Four and all their friends.

2. Start sweeping, vacuuming, or mopping from the farthest corner of the room, working backwards to the door. Otherwise, you'll need to walk over your clean floor when you've finished.

3. Always wipe up a spill as soon as you see it. Fridges, ovens, and microwaves can be really hard to clean once a stain sets. And on that note, wipe your oven and base each time after you use it.

4. Dry stainless steel as soon as you've washed it — any water left will leave a mark.

5. To get white rings off a wood table, use one of the following: petroleum jelly, olive oil, and vinegar; mayonnaise and ash mixed together (yes, really!); or "Brasso" metal polish.

A Cleaning Plan

If you stay on top of cleaning, you won't find any nasty surprises. (What is that thing growing in the corner, by the way?)

Every day

Don't panic, it's really only mainte-nance – not cleaning – and will only take a few minutes! Clean up any spills in the kitchen or on the countertops as soon as they happen; otherwise, they can become really tricky to get rid of later. Letting it cool slightly first, take 30 seconds to wipe out the oven every time you use it; otherwise, spills get baked on, and you'll need a nuclear blast to clean them up. Wipe up any mess in the microwave for the same reason. Sweep the floor when you can see that it is dusty or dirty. Do a ten-second tidy up of each room as you leave it. Clean the toilet if there's a stain. Finally, attend to any stains on carpets or drapes immediately.

> **Do a ten second tidy up of each room as you leave it**

Every week

Do the dusting, remove cobwebs, clean toilets and sinks, wipe mirrors, and mop and vacuum every week. If you've been lazy and haven't been doing it each time, wipe out the microwave and oven, then wipe the countertops, and clean the kitchen sink. Change the sheets on your bed every week or, at a stretch, every fortnight. And open some windows to give your place a good airing.

Every month

Clean out the fridge and throw away that jar of unidentifiable gunk that seems to be moving around the top shelf. Clean out the filter on the dishwasher (if you are unsure how to do this, find the instruction manual of your dishwasher online). Cleaning the filter takes about two minutes and ensures the dishwasher works effectively as well as stopping it from smelling. While you're there, put the filters of the range hood through the dishwasher. Wipe over leather upholstery with a slightly damp cloth, dust the baseboards, and polish any wood furniture. Clean one shelf per month of your pantry or food cupboard, discarding out-of-date food and wiping down the shelf.

Every year

Wash your windows. Get the carpets cleaned professionally, or do it yourself if you can borrow a carpet washer.

Wash your windows and carpets each year

Products You Need

Not many people like cleaning, so make it easier by having the right tools. You don't need to spend a fortune on cleaning equipment, but if it makes you happy, and you can afford it, go for it! At a minimum, you will need the following:

Hardware

- Broom
- Vacuum (essential if you have carpet, although can be useful for a wood floor too)
- Mop
- Mop bucket with wringer (Get one on wheels, and you will thank me every time you use it.)
- Toilet brush and stand, one per toilet
- Rubber gloves for the kitchen and one pair that you leave near each toilet
- Cloths and sponges, including some micro-fiber cloths. Have separate ones for the kitchen, for general cleaning, and for toilets.

- Cobweb brush, or at a stretch, you can try to use the broom.
- A squeegee for cleaning windows and the shower screen, or you can use scrunched up newspaper.

Cleaning products

- Toilet bowl cleaner. Choose a "duck neck" bottle shape so that you can squirt under the rim of the toilet.
- Dish detergent for the dishes
- Floor cleaner (check that it's suitable for your type of floor)
- Window cleaner (or you can use water with a splash of vinegar)
- Spray cleaner for countertops, such as an orange spray, or use hot, soapy water on a cloth
- Furniture polish if you have wood furniture
- And maybe cleaner for the shower door (or use the window cleaner).

Dusting, Wet or Dry

You should always work from top to bottom, so this means attacking dusting, cobwebs, and mirrors before you do the vacuuming and/or the mopping.

Start your cleaning session with the dusting as this means the dust you disturb will settle on the floor, ready to be mopped or vacuumed up. You can use either a duster (often a fluffy little thing) or a dusting cloth, but if you find the dust upsets the allergies of someone in your household, you can always wet-dust, using a slightly damp cloth and wiping over any surfaces. Or if you are the one who's allergic to the dust, tell your roommate you can't do it because of your health. Same with the vacuuming.

Dust or wipe all surfaces where dust may have settled, such as mantel shelves, countertops, tables, blinds, windowsills and the tops of picture frames. For cobwebs, attack with a cobweb brush — it looks like a big, flat toilet brush on a very long extendable handle. You can use a broom, but it's likely to leave dirty marks on the wall and won't reach as high as the cobweb brush.

Sweeping & Vacuuming

Hard surfaces

Make sure you sweep or vacuum your floors well before mopping. Start in the corner farthest from the door, and then work backwards towards it. You should put your vacuum on the correct setting for a hard floor — often there will be a little etched drawing on the top of the head to show you which setting is correct. If it's not on the correct setting, it can be very difficult to move along the floor and may scratch some floor surfaces.

Be thorough as any dust or grit left can scratch the floor or leave streaks once you mop.

Carpets

Again, vacuum from a corner of the room, backwards towards the door. Make sure you keep an eye on the dust container of your vacuum and empty it as required. If the suction disappears, a full vacuum is the likely problem. Or else you've sucked up the cat.

Mopping

Mop from the farthest corner of the room, back towards the door. Keep your mop in contact with the floor, going backwards and forwards in large strokes, and clean it regularly in the bucket that you bring along with you. Make sure you wring out the mop firmly before you mop, keeping the mop damp but not soaking wet. This is particularly important for wood floors, which can warp, stain, or end up streaky if too much water is applied.

Mop from the farthest corner of the room, back towards the door

Excellent cleaning products are available at the supermarket for every type of floor. These need to be diluted into your mopping bucket according to the instructions on the bottle. Alternatively, you can make your own floor cleaners at home.

- For wood floors, use warm water alone or warm water with a splash of olive oil. Do not use hot water as this can cause the floor to crack.

- For linoleum or tile, use a small amount of detergent diluted in warm water.

- For tile or stone, you can use warm water with a splash of vinegar added.

If you can, open the windows to help the floor dry, and to keep it clean, tell your idiot roommate not to walk on it till it is dry.

Bathroom

Toilet

If you use the toilet and there is a stain there after flushing (yep, I'm talking about poop here), use the brush to get rid of it, then flush again, holding the brush under the flushing water. If you don't do this, it can set hard and then be harder to remove later, particularly if it's high up on the bowl and not reached by the flushing water.

If you don't like the idea of poop on the brush, put a piece of toilet paper on the stain, and then use the brush to rub it off. The toilet paper can then be flushed down the toilet. You will still need to run the brush under the flushing water to get all the paper off. If you attend to stains as they occur, your weekly clean will be much easier.

For the weekly clean, you need to have a sponge and a pair of rubber gloves that are only used for this purpose – put them in a plastic container marked "toilet cleaning" under the bathroom sink.

Using the toilet bowl cleaner, squirt liquid under the rim all around the bowl so that it drips down the inside of the toilet. This works best if the bowl is dry, so don't do it just after you've used the toilet. I like to use enough cleaner so that I almost cover the inside of the bowl with the drips. Leave it for at least five minutes.

Using the toilet brush, dip the brush into the water and scrub away the liquid, dipping into the water and scrubbing below the water line. Scrub all of the bowl, including under the rim. Finally, flush the toilet and hold the toilet brush under the spray. Put it back into the holder. Now, wearing your gloves, use the sponge to wipe over the seat, both on top and underneath. You can put some toilet bowl cleaner on the sponge if you like, spray it with some spray cleaner, or just use it as is. There are also disposable toilet-cleaning wipes available, which the manufacturers say are flushable (I'm not too sure), although they are expensive and don't necessarily do a better job than cleaning with a sponge.

Rinse the sponge in the water in the toilet. You do know that this water is cleaner than some water you drink, don't you? You may find this hard to believe, but in a study in Britain, the ice served in six out of ten chain restaurants had more bacteria than the water in their toilets.[24] If you can't bear rinsing the sponge in the toilet, use the sink. Wring the sponge out and store with the gloves under the sink.

Bathroom sink

Sinks get grimy from soap residue and toothpaste, so make sure you clean them every week at least. Use a spray or liquid cleaner on a sponge, keeping this sponge only for use on the sink. Once you have wiped over the whole sink, rinse out the sponge and wipe over it again, removing all traces of the cream or spray. Finally, dry the sink with a dishtowel that will then go into a hot wash.

Bathtub & shower recess

Bathtubs and showers should be wiped over once a week as well. If you want to be environmentally aware, you can use a micro-fiber cloth designed for the purpose. You could also use baking soda and vinegar, or just use shower spray and be done with it.

If you have mold problems, you can use a couple of drops of clove oil in a liter of warm water and use it to wipe down the problem areas. Clove oil kills mold. There are also commercial mold killer products available.

Bedroom

Changing your sheets

People have different ideas about this, but while the general rule has always been every week, you can probably get away with changing your sheets every second week if you're not a real slob. It can make things easier if you use two sheets and sleep between them, with the duvet on top. This means that you only need to wash your duvet cover every month or so as it is not in contact with your body.

Kitchen

Stovetop

Always wipe down the stovetop as soon as you've spilled something. The heat from the burner bakes it on, and it's a pain to remove later. If you haven't listened to this advice, then put a dripping wet cloth on the blob while you do something else for a few minutes. You should then be able to wipe it up easily, but if not, then try again. If you're in the mood for some extra cleaning, you can take off any removable parts around the burners and soak them in hot soapy water.

Oven

I've said earlier that you should wipe out the oven every time you use it. Okay, so you've forgotten a few (like 20) times, and now it's filthy. There are industrial strength cleaners you can buy at the store, but these are pretty toxic, which doesn't seem a great idea to me for an

Wipe out the oven every time you use it

appliance that cooks my food. Alternatively, you can call a company that will come and clean your oven while separating you from an enormous amount of money.

Case Study:

Oven Cleaning

Michael moved into a new apartment with his buddies. His parents had taught him well about cooking a roast, and he loved to throw one in the oven on a Sunday night for his friends. He hated cleaning his oven and didn't do it.

After three years (and 150 roasts), the time came to move out of the apartment, and he found that the oven was so bad that he had to have it professionally cleaned before he could get his deposit back. It cost $170, which he couldn't afford.

Lesson: Wipe out your oven each time you use it.

If paying someone to clean your oven isn't in your budget, you can search online for an environmentally friendly method. Often these use a paste of baking soda and water that you apply, leave on overnight, and then remove with a wet cloth. Next spray with vinegar and watch the remnants of the baking soda go bananas with bubbling, just like those model volcanoes you used to make in elementary school. A razor blade scraper can be great for really hard to remove grime. This method is said to work, but I would still highly recommend the "thirty seconds each time" method of wiping it out every time you've used it. Make sure you wait till it cools down first.

Range hood

Take off the filters, and put them through the dishwasher — they will come out like new! Wipe the outside of the range hood — wow, how did it get so grubby?

Microwave

What? It's dirty? Okay, so you're not perfect, and you weren't wiping it out every time you used it. Now it's vile, so wash the turntable with hot soapy water or put it in the dishwasher, and wipe out the inside of the microwave with a damp cloth. Don't forget the ceiling of the microwave; you may have to bend down to see it.

Sink

Sinks can get pretty mucky, so wring out a micro-fiber cloth in hot soapy water, making sure it's almost dry. Wipe over all the surfaces, and keep washing and wringing out the cloth to keep it clean as you wipe. Dry it with a dishtowel to make it look really clean. You can get stainless steel cleaners, but I'm not sure they're worth it for a sink. See *Stainless Steel* on following page.

Pantry

If you've been putting all your open food into containers, you shouldn't have a moth problem. Choose a shelf, and take out all the food. Wipe it over, throw away any out-of-date food, and wash any containers that need it. Put it all back, and admire your handiwork! Do a different shelf every month, and you'll keep on top of it.

Other Cleaning Issues

Stainless steel

Stainless steel looks oh so stylish! But it can be a pain to keep clean, with fingerprints causing a particular problem. To clean it, you can use a micro-fiber cloth with plain water, but make sure you dry it well as watery spots can leave more marks. If this is not working well for you, you can buy a very effective stainless steel spray, or you can also use glass cleaner or white vinegar in water (the latter works well for glass as well). Make sure you rinse the surface you are cleaning after you use these products; then dry with a dishtowel.

Wood furniture

For modern wood furniture, make sure that you keep it well dusted and look after it while you use it. Don't put items on it that will scratch (or if you do, use a coaster underneath), put a saucer under plants that could leak, and try to keep the item out of

Never leave wet towels on wood furniture

the sun as this will cause fading. Never leave wet towels or clothing on wood furniture as they will leave a water mark. And if you spill something on a wood table during dinner, always wipe it up quickly.

To clean wood furniture, use a good quality wood polish, rub it in with a clean soft cloth, and then buff with another soft cloth. Make sure you follow the manufacturer's instructions and don't use too much as it can leave a greasy finish, which will attract dust. Sprays give a good result but can end up leaving a layer that can be hard to remove once it builds up.

Some furniture will have had a special finish applied, which means it will only require a quick wipe with a damp cloth, and any oil that you put on will just serve to make it greasy. To check whether your furniture has this finish, you can just apply a small amount of polish on an inconspicuous area and see what happens. If it is absorbed, it's okay to use the polish. If it beads (like water on the sink), the furniture will just need a wipe with a slightly damp cloth and to be dried with a dishtowel.

For antique wood furniture, my advice is to be very careful! Buy a polish specifically for antiques, preferably one with beeswax, and use it sparingly, buffing well to remove it.

To remove white rings from glasses on wood, there are several different methods:

- Rub petroleum jelly into the stain, leave overnight, and rub off.
- Use olive oil and vinegar mixed together to rub off the stain.
- Continuing in the salad theme, you can use mayonnaise mixed with a little ash to rub off the mark.
- Or strangely, use "Brasso" metal polish and rub from the outside of the stain to the inside.

Window cleaning

If you can, avoid cleaning windows on really hot days — the glass dries too quickly, and it may streak.

Firstly, vacuum around the window frames (inside) and (if you can reach) brush with a dry brush (outside); then wipe the frames both inside and out with a damp soapy cloth. To clean the glass, commercial window cleaning sprays are very effective but not always necessary. If the windows are very dirty, first clean them with warm, soapy water and a soft brush. Then use glass cleaning spray or clean water with a some vinegar, dishwasher powder, or rubbing alcohol added. A squeegee will remove all the water and prevent streaking of the glass as it dries as will a ball of plain newspaper scrunched up and rubbed over the glass to dry it.

Wood Blinds

These are tricky little stinkers to clean, but if you put socks over your hands and run them between the blades, it can work miracles! If they are in a really bad state and you have access to an outside area, unclip them and take them outside, where you can scrub them with hot soapy water then rinse off.

Five Top Tips

1. If you're going to buy a bucket for mopping, buy one on wheels. It may be low on your list of priorities, but it will make mopping a joy (almost).

2. Start your cleaning up high with dusting, cobwebs, and cleaning of mirrors, and work your way down low to vacuuming and mopping.

3. Clove oil kills mold. Add a few drops to a liter of water, and wipe anything that is looking dicey.

4. Anything wet left on wood will leave a white mark. If you do leave something wet on wood, take it off immediately, and dry the wood with a dishtowel.

5. Don't clean windows on a hot day. They'll end up streaky.

CHAPTER 9

That's My Car!

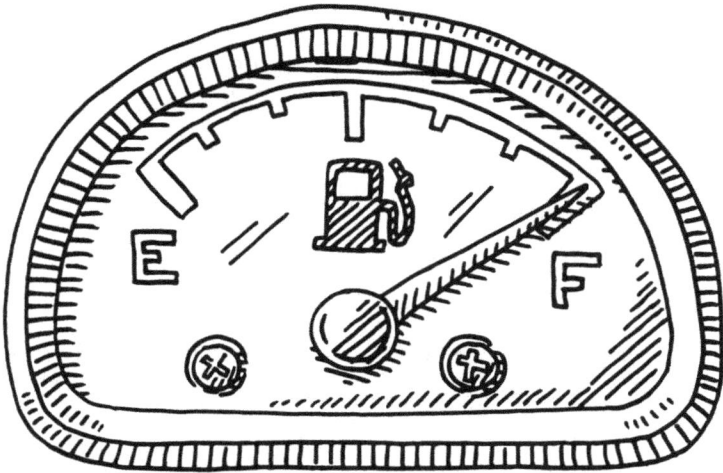

W hen it comes to thinking about cars, there are a few things you
need to know...

Haven't Got Time to Read the Whole Chapter?
Read This.

1. The safest cars have side-curtain air bags, Electronic Stability Control (ESC), Anti-lock Braking System (ABS) brakes, and seatbelt pre-tensioners.[25]

2. White is the safest car color — it is involved in fewer accidents, and if you do have an accident, it is associated with a less severe outcome.

3. To purchase your car, save as much as possible and borrow as little as possible. Look for a low interest rate, and then repay the loan as quickly as you can.

4. Air pressure in tires is important. You should check it when the tires are cold and increase it for heavy loads or high speeds.

5. While parking tickets don't give you points on your license, moving violations like speeding, texting while driving, and drinking while driving do. If you get too many, you'll lose your license, not to mention increase your risk of being seriously hurt in an accident. Points also increase your annual insurance rates.

Budgeting for Your Car

Apart from your house, your car is likely to be the biggest asset you'll buy. Cars are expensive! You will need to do your math to work out how much that cool little vehicle will actually cost you to buy and then to run.

How much does a car cost?

In planning your car budget, you'll need to add in the cost of the following items:

- Purchase price of the car or repayments for your car loan
- Insurance premiums
- Registration & taxes
- Gas
- Maintenance
- Tires
- Repairs, if you need them

Cars are expensive to run. Think insurance, registration, gas, maintenance and repairs

If you look on the *AAA* website, you will see how much it can cost to own a car. The average in 2015 was $8698 per year.[26]

If you'd rather see a cost per mile, and assuming that you're driving about 10,000 miles per year, you will see that, for example, a small sedan (such as a Chevrolet Cruze, Ford Focus, Honda Civic, Hyundai Elantra, or Toyota Corolla) will cost you about 58 cents for every mile you drive. If you look at a medium-sized sedan (such as a Chevrolet Malibu, Ford Fusion, Honda Accord, Nissan Altima, or Toyota Camry), you'll be looking at about 76 cents per mile. And if you have a gas-guzzler such as a Buick LaCrosse, Chrysler 300, Ford Taurus, Nissan Maxima, or Toyota Avalon, the price will be about 93 cents per mile.

All these prices are for new cars and include a component for depreciation (an annual decrease in its value) and finance, so if you buy an older (read: cheaper) car, these costs will be much less. The lesson? Decrease your finance costs by saving up before you buy, and then buy second-hand and small.

Buying Your Car

Safety

Think carefully about the type of car you buy, particularly in terms of safety. There is a worldwide system that rates new cars on their safety, and in the U.S. it is the NHTSA/IIHS.[27] One star is the worst rating, and five stars is the best. You are twice as likely to be killed or seriously injured in a one-star rated car as a five-star rated car.

According to the World Health Organization, worldwide car accidents are the highest cause of premature death for 15- to 29-year-olds worldwide.[28] If your budget allows it, always try to buy a car with side airbags, Electronic Stability Control (ESC), seatbelt pre-tensioners, and Anti-lock Braking System (ABS) brakes. It's worthwhile referring to www.safercar.gov[29] to look at the safety of cars you might be considering.

Color

According to Monash University,[30] white is the safest color in terms of crash risk, particularly during the daytime. They also say that if a crash does occur, there's the likelihood you'll be less injured in a white car than in any other color car. One other thing to remember about the color of your car: Red fades more than other colors. So if you do buy a red car, particularly an older one, make sure you wax it regularly to provide a protective layer.

White is the safest color in terms of crash risk

Size

Buy a small car with a small engine, locally made or assembled (or at least not European), and don't modify it. Avoid a sporty car. Insurance companies believe small cars have fewer accidents, and so they charge the cheapest insurance premiums for them.

What is the safest car?

- NHTSA: 5 stars
- Color: white
- With: Side-curtain airbags
- Features: ABS and ESC

Age

You'll need to think about the age of the car you want to buy. There are some excellent used cars around, and they are obviously much cheaper than new ones, so it pays to do your homework. Check how your potential purchase ranks in safety, and of course get it checked by your local mechanic, but don't discount it just because it's old and not very cool.

Paying for Your Car

Make sure you have thought about how you will finance your car before you go looking for it. Ideally you will have been saving dutifully — clearly it's best if you wait until you can pay cash and then buy what you can afford without a loan. If you haven't got cash, you need to do some serious planning now.

Be very careful about taking out a loan from the car dealer. It is extremely tricky to work out what the final cost will be even if you are

Be careful taking a loan from a car dealer

assured there is "zero interest." This interest rate may be for a limited time, and then the interest rate reverts to one that is very high. There are also other charges that may be added. Car dealers bank on you being carried away with the delight of a quick purchase — and sign you up to a loan that may have significant drawbacks. Do your due diligence. Get on to a car loan comparison website to get the best deal.

And have you explored other options, like your loving family? Perhaps they may be prepared to loan you at least part of the money. To maintain harmonious familial relationships, you need to establish a payback schedule and stick to it.

How to Buy a Car

Visit some websites

The *Autotrader* website is a good place to start as it will give you prices for both new and used cars from dealers and for cars being sold privately. You already know new cars lose value very quickly once they leave the dealership, so if you want more bang for your buck, you'd be better off buying a used car and buying it privately. Privately sold cars are cheaper than those from dealers, and besides, you know car salesmen in car lots are notoriously dicey.

Many used cars are under warranty till they are five years old — look at the manufacturer's websites as warranty periods differ from car company to car company. But it's worth noting here that while the manufacturer's warranty passes on to the next owner, if the person selling the car has purchased an extended warranty, it does not pass on to you.

A great option is to buy a known car from a family friend because they are likely to be more honest with you about the history of the car. If someone has the type of car you are after, ask if they are planning to upgrade or sell — you never know unless you ask.

Test drive some cars

First of all, be prepared to look at lots of cars till you find the right one. When you do find a car that you like, arrange for a test drive. If you can, drive on a variety of roads, including local suburban streets and freeways to test the car at various speeds and both during the day and at night. Bring a friend along who might notice something that you do not (and even better if they are a car enthusiast).

Negotiate the price

If you are happy with the car, negotiate the price. First of all, look up the value on *Kelley Blue Book*[31] to see what the car is really worth. In the case of a private sale, make sure that the seller understands that you will only proceed if there is a satisfactory vehicle check. You should offer a significant discount to their asking price – say 20% –

Check your car's value on *Kelley Blue Book*

and with any luck, you may end up with a 10% discount, particularly with a privately sold car. Stand your ground – remember, there are lots of cars out there, and they are just as eager to sell as you are to buy!

Check the history of the car

You'll want to know about the history of the car and, in particular, whether it has been written off after a severe crash, stolen, or has money owed against it. The first means that it could be dicey mechanically; the other two mean that it could be taken away from you even if you've paid for it.

By using the Vehicle Identification Number, or VIN, (found on the inside of the car door, on the registration papers, or on the engine – and they should all match), you can pay for a search to be done of a number of national databases, which will give you this information. At the time of writing, the most prominent companies were charging about $20, but with some Internet crawling, you can get a report for less than $10. Just type *VIN check* into your Internet search engine.

Cooling-off period - there isn't one!

A cooling-off period allows you to cancel a contract of sale if you change your mind. But note this well: There is no cooling-off period on car sales — either privately or from a dealer. Once you sign that contract, the car is yours, so think hard before you sign.

Attend to the nitty gritty

Once the price has been agreed on, get the car checked out by a mechanic. Many organizations offer this service, but a good place to start is by googling *automobile inspections.* If you are buying from a dealer, you can skip this step as they will offer you a warranty.

Read up on the details of *How to Register Your Car* below. On the day of the transaction, arrange for a cover note for insurance (later in this chapter), make sure that the paperwork is complete, then pay your money. Do not pay until the required paperwork has been completed, and make sure you get a receipt for the money you have paid.

And don't forget to join the American Automobile Association (AAA)[32]. Each year the AAA helps more than 29 million stranded drivers by doing things like changing flat tires and providing assistance with vehicle lockout, battery jump starts, and emergency fuel. It's not for profit, and it's just one less thing to worry about if you have them on your side. Just remember that AAA membership is not transferable, and to get assistance, you need to have a membership card. It won't help if other members of your family are members or if you borrow a car whose owner is a member; to get help, you need to join yourself. AAA membership will cost about $60 per year plus a joining fee. This will entitle you to a number of benefits, including cheap travel and discounted car repairs.

An alternative that offers fewer benefits but which can be cheaper if you just want mechanical help on the side of the road is to look at the roadside assistance that your car insurer offers. It can be less than $20 per year.

How to Register Your Car

If you buy from a dealer, the car registration will be handled for you.

If you buy from a private seller, you will need to change over the certificate of ownership (or title) of the car into your name.

Because car registration is handled differently in each state, there are variations depending on where you are based. In some states, the car will need to have a safety inspection before the registration is transferred. Other states require odometer statements, satisfactory air pollution controls, or proof of insurance. Note that some states might charge a higher fee if you are registering an out-of-state vehicle.

This seems very complex, but finding out the procedure in your state is actually quite easy. Look at *Title Transfer of Ownership* on the *Digest of Motor Laws* website.[33] It is extremely comprehensive and lists state-by-state details for 51 other motor laws as well — a nice little bit of bedtime reading for you!

Insurance

Make sure you insure your car from the moment you first take possession of it. You can arrange for a cover note (temporary insurance) from your insurance company over the phone or the Internet.

How to insure your car

Things you will need to know to take out insurance include the following:

- The make of your car (e.g., Toyota)
- The model (e.g., Corolla)
- The year of manufacture of the car
- Whether there are any added extras (e.g., tow bars, anti-theft devices, etc.)

Insure in whose name?

Think about whether you will have the car insured in your name or in a parent's name.

If it is in your name, insurance will be more expensive because younger drivers have more accidents. You will also be sure that your car will be covered while you are driving, whatever the circumstances.

If your parents insure your car in their names, the insurance will be cheaper. However, if your parents don't tell the insurance company you are the main driver of the car, you may not be covered in the case of an accident. If they are up front about who is driving the car and include your car on their own policy, it will jack up the cost of their insurance enormously.

Decide what type of insurance you want

There are different levels of car insurance you can take out (in order from cheapest to most expensive):

1. Liability for Bodily Injury (BI) – insurance that covers costs relating to an injury that your car causes to another person (e.g., if you run over your neighbor and you break their leg)

2. Liability for Property Damage (PD) – insurance that covers damage to other cars or property by your car (e.g. the damage caused if your car runs into your neighbor's fence and destroys it)

3. Full Coverage – This covers both BI and PD above as well as damage to your own car.

You will also need to decide if you want to add any extras, such as windshield replacement and roadside assistance – which come at a cost of course!

Decide what deductible you want

A deductible is the part of every claim that you yourself must pay before the insurance company kicks in the rest. Yes, this sounds strange, but it is one way insurance companies have of avoiding

> **You can decrease your premium by increasing the deductible**

frivolous claims. You can decrease your premium (the amount you pay each year for insurance) by increasing the deductible, so for instance, you may get a 20% discount on the premium by increasing your deductible from $600 to $1,100. In this case, it means that it is not worth your while to make a claim for anything worth less than $1,100.

Compare premiums

It is easy to take out insurance online, and it is worth getting onto a comparison website to find the cheapest insurance available. There will be a wide range of prices for similar insurance. This is because some companies actively discourage younger drivers, while some companies are prepared to accept them as part of their overall insurance portfolio. It is therefore worth shopping around for the insurer that fits your particular needs, so spend some time online to find the best deal for you and your car.

What to Do if You Have an Accident

Look after people first

Immediately check that all passengers are okay. If not, call the emergency service. As you know, this is 911 in the U.S. (and if you're interested, it's 999 in the U.K. and 112 in Europe). You will be asked what sort of problem it is and therefore whether you need police, fire, or ambulance, and clearly, at this stage, you want ambulance. Be prepared to tell them where you are (they will most likely know if you are using a home phone but may not know if you are on your cell phone), which crossroad is the closest, and what has happened. Do not hang up until they tell you to do so.

Make sure that you and other passengers are safe and not in a position where you and they may be hurt by other vehicles. If possible, move your car to a position where it is not obstructing traffic and does not pose a risk to other drivers. Do not endanger yourself by doing this.

If the damage is over $500, if someone has been injured, or the other driver flees the scene, you may need to file a police report. Check your local laws.

Get down the details

Speak to the other driver, if there is one, and make a record of the following:

- Their name and contact number
- The make, model, color, and registration of their car

Photographing their license and the damaged car(s) and license plates is an easy way of doing this.

If there are witnesses, get their contact details as well. This will be useful if there is a dispute about culpability.

Move your car

If your car if drivable, call to see if you can find a friend to come without their own car to drive you and your car home so that you don't have to drive yourself. The high levels of adrenaline in your body resulting from an accident

High levels of adrenaline after an accident can impair your decision-making sills

can impair your decision-making skills and make it dangerous for you to drive home.

If your car is not drivable, you will need to call your insurance company. If there is a dispute about who is at fault, call the police and request their attendance — they will produce an incident report that can subsequently be called upon by the insurance companies at a later date.

Submit your claim...

Some insurance companies have an app where you can submit photographs directly from your smart phone via the app to start the claims process. You can download it on the spot and start the claims process on the side of the road.

If the damage is large and you haven't yet contacted your insurance company, when you get home, compose yourself, then call them or contact them through their website. You don't need to know your policy number — they can search for your name or your car's license plate. You should do this whether it is you or the other person who is at fault. They will handle it from there on in.

...or arrange your own repairs

But if your car is only slightly damaged and it's not worth going through the insurance company, make sure you get several quotes for repairs from body shops or mechanics. There can be a wide range of prices charged for the same repairs.

And a word about driving and the law

Driving laws are administered by each state and are not designed to increase revenue for the government but to decrease risky driving (yes, really!). Speeding is a common reason to be pulled over by the police, and this is because an increase in speed is correlated with an increase in accidents. If you drive at three mph above the speed limit of 35 mph, you double your chance of being involved in an accident resulting in a casualty.[34]

Further, according to the NHTSA, in 2012, 28% of young drivers involved in fatal accidents had been drinking and 55% of 15- to 20-year-olds killed in accidents were unrestrained,[35] while every day 11 teenagers are killed when driving and texting.[36]

If you are caught breaking the law while driving, you will incur demerit points and a fine. Depending on what the violation is, you may be able to go to "traffic school," after which the points will be wiped clean from your record and will not be reported to your insurance company. Otherwise, a report will be made to your insurance company, and your insurance rates will go up.

If you earn too many demerit points, you will lose your license. For more serious infractions, a judge can suspend your license in court. Be careful — all this information can feed into your insurance company and can affect your premiums.

Local municipalities administer parking infringements, and you do not incur demerit points for these — just a pesky fine. These can totally destroy your budget, so always check the parking sign carefully when you stop your car.

You also need to be familiar with the laws in your state, so get on to the *Digest of Motor Laws* on the *AAA* website. You'll find out all the laws (plus many, many more) that relate to:

- Blood-alcohol content (BAC)
- Use of a cell phone, including hands-free devices
- Curfews for different aged drivers
- Speed limits
- Pollution control

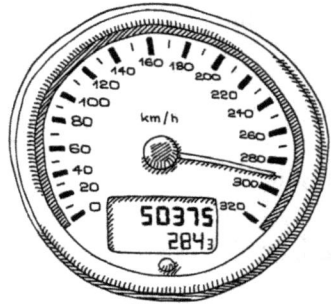

How to Maintain Your Car

Cleaning your car

You should clean your car at least once a month. Either go to one of those car wash places and have fun with a couple of dollars and a high pressure hose or do it at home using the following method.

Inside

Clean the inside of the car first. Take out the rubber mats and wash them in warm, soapy water, and leave them standing vertically to dry. Throw away any trash you find inside the car. Vacuum the carpet and the seats using a long, thin vacuum attachment so that you can get into all the nooks and crannies and around the pedals. If you can, use your normal vacuum cleaner rather than a hand-held one – the latter doesn't have enough power to do a really good job. Put on the soft brush attachment, and vacuum the dashboard.

You can use plastic cleaner to clean the dashboard and leather cleaner for leather seats, but warm, soapy water on a very well wrung-out cloth can be a good alternative. Be careful as too much water can be a disaster for electrical components if it seeps through. It's not that great for fabric seats either, so be careful and wring out your cloth well.

Wipe the rear-view mirror, and clean the inside of all the windows. You're done. Now on to the outside.

Outside

This is much easier at a self-service car wash. If that's not possible, here's one way to do it at home. Spray the outside of your car well with a hose; then use a soft brush or a sponge and warm soapy water in a bucket to clean the whole of the car, starting at the top and working down. If you're using a sponge, make sure you wring it out before putting it back in the bucket to avoid dirtying the water.

Hose the whole car down again to remove loosened dirt and suds, and then squeegee the windows clean. Finally, dry the whole car, either with a chamois or a couple of old towels. You can put some polish on after this, which basically involves putting it on and rubbing it off using quite a lot of physical effort — read the instructions on the bottle. You can also use some tire spray to make the tires black — looks very gangsta!

Tire care

- Most states have a legal requirement that tires have tread of at least 2/32 of an inch, so if the tread gets down to 3/32 of an inch, start looking for tires. Alternatively, (and remember, it's not entirely accurate), there is the "penny test." Insert a penny upside down into the tread, with President Lincoln's head going in head first. If you can see his whole head, it's time to buy new tires! Why is tread important? It's because when tread wears, it takes longer for you to stop and you handle corners with less control.

- Make sure you have the right inflation pressure for your tire. Look for the manufacturer's recommended pressure on the sticker on the driver's side door pillar or fuel flap.

- Check your tire pressure when your tires are cold. Increase pressure for heavy loads or sustained high speeds.

- Like everything, tires age — check the tire's age by looking at the Tire Identification Number (TIN). The last four digits indicate the week and year the tire was made (e.g., a tire with TIN XXX4816 was made in the 48th week of 2016.

Check your tire pressure when your tires are cold

- Rotate your tires regularly and at least every 3,000 to 5,000 miles. Rotating tires means that they wear evenly.

- Get a professional wheel alignment every six months. A worn tire increases the time it takes to brake on wet roads.

Your car will handle better and use less gas when the tires have the correct inflation pressure. Your car handbook will tell you what this pressure should be (or a quick search of the Internet will do the same). Every gas station will have an air hose to refill your tires. Unscrew the little cap on your tire, push on the far end of the metal hand piece until it seals, then read the pressure off the dial. If the pressure is too low, depress the lever without disconnecting the hand piece from the tire. (On some hoses, you do not need to depress a lever — air will be added automatically.)

Don't forget to screw on the little plastic cap again!

How to open the hood

Make sure the ignition is off and the car is parked on a flat surface with the handbrake on. If you've never done this before, it is a two-step process. You need to undo the latch while you are still seated inside the car — it is usually around knee height on the door side, but if you can't find it, check your owner's manual. You will need to pull it firmly and will hear a click outside. Then go to the front of the car, where you will notice that the hood is now slightly ajar. Standing directly in front of the car (in the middle), slide your hand in between the hood and the car, depress the little lever you will feel, and while still depressing it, lift the hood. Some hoods will need the long stick that is lying horizontally at the front of the engine to stay open — it will fit into an opening underneath the hood and hold it up. Other hoods will stay up by themselves.

How to check the water

The radiator is one of the main parts of the cooling system of your car and contains liquid that circulates through the system (i.e., "coolant"). If you see the high temperature warning display on your dashboard, stop driving and take care of it immediately.

Before checking anything under the hood of the car, it is good practice to familiarize yourself with the engine bay layout by reading the owner's manual that comes with your car.

If your car is fitted with an expansion tank (a plastic coolant reservoir), check that the coolant level is at — or slightly above — the "minimum" mark when the engine is cold or somewhere between the half and "maximum" marks with the engine at normal (hot) operating temperature.

If your car is not fitted with an expansion tank (typically older vehicles), check that the coolant (or water) is within about one inch of the top of the filler neck when the engine is cold. Never attempt this with a hot car as the radiator contents are under pressure and you could end up with boiling water or hot coolant spurting in your face. To check the level, unscrew the radiator lid, which is found near the front of the engine. If it is an original lid, it will often be yellow and marked with words such as "engine coolant," "under pressure," or "caution." Sometimes these lids are lost and are then replaced with plastic ones that may or may not have any markings on them. The shape of the lid is usually round with a projection on either side.

Take the lid off and look inside — you should be able to see the fluid right near the top. If more coolant is required, use a mixture of clean water and the recommended coolant/inhibitor. Make sure you screw the lid back on again.

Persistent coolant loss indicates a problem, which your mechanic should check immediately.

Persistent coolant loss indicates a problem

Case Study:

Attending to Maintenance

Nicholas notices the temperature gauge on his car is heading towards "high." It's rush hour, he's in a hurry, and his girlfriend will be furious if he is late...again. He decides to risk it and keeps on driving the 30 minutes to her house.

The car temperature gauge rises. His car overheats, and smoke starts coming out from under his hood. He pulls over, and after the car is towed to the garage, he discovers he's now got head gasket issues. By not stopping to do a five-minute job and refilling his radiator, he has a big problem on his hands now.

Lesson: Always attend to car maintenance issues promptly.

How to check the oil

Cars need oil to reduce the friction between the moving parts and to help dissipate the heat caused by normal workings of the engine. If you don't keep the oil level up, things can go badly wrong.

To check the oil, open the hood (as noted above). Locate the oil dipstick, which is a metal stick inserted deep into the engine — all you will see is a little finger-sized metal or

plastic loop that is sticking out. Pull the stick out, wipe it off with a cloth, reinsert it, and pull it out again. Look at the level the oil has reached on the stick. The bottom end of the stick will have markings on it to indicate what level the engine oil is at – often with an "L" (for low) on one end of the markings and an "H" (for high) on the other. The level should be up towards the "H."

If it is down towards the "L," start by adding a liter of oil. Buy the oil that is recommended in your owner's manual (they come in different grades). To add oil, unscrew the oil cap located on top of the engine and typically marked with "OIL" or a picture of an oil can, and pour in the oil, either with a funnel or straight out of the oil can. Now check the oil again to see that the level has risen and is now okay. If not, add more oil. Voila! Done!

How to change a tire

If you are a member of a motoring association or have paid your insurance company for roadside assistance, they will do this for you. Call them and wait.

If you aren't a member, are in a rush, or just want to do it yourself, do the following:

1. Make sure the car is parked safely away from the line of traffic on a flat piece of ground. Do not change a tire on a hill.

2. Put the parking brake on, and turn on the hazard lights.

3. Get the spare tire out of the trunk.

4. Find the tools in the trunk of the car, and use the flat end of the wrench to lever off the hubcap if there is one; then use the socket end of the wrench to just loosen each of the tire bolts. Do not take them off at this stage.

5. Locate the jack in the trunk of the car, align it under the chassis of the car at the point indicated in the car's manual, and jack it up till the tire clears the ground.

6. Now completely loosen all the bolts, each bolt a little at a time (i.e., not one bolt completely then the others). Put the bolts in the upturned hubcap or in a pile together on the ground.

7. Gently pull the tire straight towards you, and lay it on the ground.

8. Pick up the spare tire, and push it on as far as it can go.

9. Gently put on each of the bolts by hand (each one a little at a time, doing ones opposite each other in turn), and then tighten with the socket end of the wrench.

10. Lower the jack carefully, and tighten all the bolts completely with the wrench, again opposites in turn.

11. Replace the hubcap, and put the flat tire in the trunk. Put the tools back in the car, and check that you haven't left anything on the ground.

12. In the next day or so, have the tire repaired. Don't drive around for weeks with a flat tire in the trunk as it's a sure invitation to get another one. And if it's a temporary space saver tire, check the manual for restrictions — usually a limited number of miles, a lower maximum speed, and no towing.

It's worth noting here that some tires on more modern cars are designed to be driven while they are flat. In this case, there is no spare tire, and the tire will last long enough to allow you to drive to a tire repair store.

Don't drive around for weeks with a flat tire

How to deal with a scratch

So someone's keyed your car while you were in the grocery store. What a pain. Grab some nail polish in the same color as your car (or white-out if it's white), and carefully paint in the scratch. From a distance and with a squint, it might look as good as new.

Another method is slightly more involved and will end up with a better result but will only work if you can't see any primer or, even worse, bare metal in the scratch. If so, forget it and revert to the first option above, or get the panel professionally resprayed.

Wash the scratch with soapy water, and then sand it with very fine (minimum 2000 grit) wet and dry sandpaper and lots of water till the scratch and the surrounding metal are at the at same level. Then use a liquid buffing compound on a cloth to get rid of any scratches left by the sandpaper, and hand buff with a soft cloth. Finally, use car wax to seal it.

Okay, let's be realistic here, neither method will be perfect, but it should look better than it did…

Maintenance

Maintenance is a pain in the neck and is also expensive. But maintaining your car means that it is safe and will last longer, and it uses less gas which is good for the environment and also your budget. In addition, a complete service book will mean your car will be more appealing to a potential buyer when you decide to upgrade.

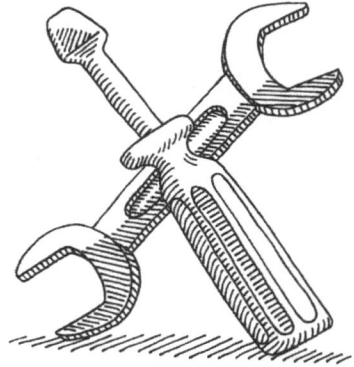

But you don't have to get your maintenance done at the dealer. Make a couple of calls to find the cheapest option. And make sure you check in your car manual when your car needs to be serviced, and don't just go by what the mechanic tells you. It can be less often than they recommend.

Gas, the environment and you

This is not the most exciting of topics, and if you are reading this, congratulations for getting this far! Everyone hates filling up the tank, and the emissions from your car are not great for the environment so to minimize your gas usage, help save the planet and save yourself a few pennies:

- Accelerate and brake smoothly.

- Drop a few mph off your speed.

- Don't carry excess baggage in your trunk (such as skis or golf clubs).

- Keep your tires at the manufacturer-recommended tire pressure.

- Make any friends who regularly ride in your car lose weight. (Not really — I just added this in to see if you were still reading.)

- Take off roof racks or luggage pods when not in use.

- Keep your car well maintained.

- Walk or ride your bike and use your car less. Good for the environment, good for your health.

Five Top Tips

1. Look at the NHTSA star rating for the safety of any car you are thinking of buying.

2. Do a search on the VIN (Vehicle Identification Number) to see if it's been stolen, has been written off, or has money owing against it.

3. If you are involved in an accident, use your phone to photograph the license of the other person, their number plate, and any damage to the cars.

4. Take out AAA membership for roadside assistance including changing flat tires, vehicle lockout, battery jump starts, and emergency fuel. An alternative is your insurance provider as they often have roadside mechanical help as part of the insurance deal.

5. Use nail polish to disguise a scratch and white-out if your car is white. It won't be perfect but looks better than nothing and protects the car from rusting until you choose to get it repaired.

CHAPTER 10

There's Something Furry Living With Us

Y ou've grown up with a dog and a couple of cats at home, and your new place seems empty without a pet. Your landlord says it's okay, but before you jump in and buy your very own Rover or Tiger, there are a few things to consider.

Haven't Got Time to Read the Whole Chapter? Read This.

1. Pets require a huge commitment of time — think 10 years for the average pet and double that for some. What will you be doing in twenty years' time?

2. Be aware that some breeds are "cheap to own," while others have inherent problems. Can you cope with a depressed American Shorthair cat or a poodle with glaucoma?

3. Houses can be dangerous places for pets — aspirin, chocolate, onions, Tylenol, aloe, and some other plants are all toxic to both dogs and cats.

4. Got $20,000 in your pocket? That's what you could be looking at to own a dog over its lifetime.

5. If you go away, cats can stay happily at home alone for up to a week if they are fed and watered; dogs are not happy at all if left alone for any length of time.

The average pet lives for 8–11 years

Thinking of Getting a Pet?

If you're thinking about buying a little fluffy companion, make sure you sit down and think carefully. Think about the commitment of time that a pet requires (feeding, exercising, and health care) as well as the significant commitment in money.

You'll also need to consider whether a pet will fit into your lifestyle (Do you travel a lot? Do you stay out late at night?) and your living space (Will your property manager allow pets?). Do your research before you jump in, and remember that pets can live for a long time. The Pet MD says that the average pet lives for 8–11 years, but some smaller pets can live for up to 20 years.[37]

Imagine you buy a pet when you are single and in your 20s. Theoretically, by the time your dog is reaching the end of its life you could be in your 40s and living a totally different lifestyle.

Case Study:
A Dog Is for Life

Morgan bought her Chihuahua puppy Clover when she was 22 years old, single, and living in an apartment. When she got married at 31, Clover was still a sprightly nine-year-old, and by the time Clover was at the end of her life, Morgan was 42 and had three children in school.

What will you be doing in 20 years? Will your pet still suit you and your lifestyle then?

Lesson: Think of the future when buying a pet.

Breed

Go online and look at the pets out there — there are all sorts of breeds with all sorts of different characteristics, and one may be perfect for you. You should bear in mind that many breeds have particular health problems e.g., Bulldogs can have respiratory problems, German Shepherds can have hip problems, Labrador Retrievers get fat, Golden Retrievers get skin allergies, and Poodles get Glaucoma. With cats, Birmans become overweight, Persians have heart problems, Abyssinians have stress-related hair loss, and American Shorthairs get depressed! Choose carefully, and don't be swayed by their cute little faces.

Where do you get your pet?

Either buy your pet from a breeder or from a shelter or rescue center. With a breeder, you are sure of what you are getting, and the breeder is as concerned as you are that the relationship works. In fact, they may want to check you out as much as you want to check them out! Pets bought from breeders can cost anywhere from a couple hundred dollars to several thousand.

If you buy from a shelter or rescue center, you will feel good that you are saving a dog or cat's life, but remember that there may have been issues that caused the pet to be abandoned in the first place. If you decide this is a good option for you, look at the *Adoptapet*[38] website. It lists thousands of available pets from shelters and rescues across the country ranging in price from as little as $25 to about $350, depending on whether you are after a cat or a dog and the age of the animal.

Don't ever buy from...

Whatever you do, there are two places where you should not buy a pet. The first is from a pet store as these pets were probably bred on a puppy farm. Their mother has most likely spent her whole life either gestating or lactating in terrible conditions. Apart from the moral issues of supporting this type of puppy production, you have no guarantee about the nature or health of the ensuing puppy, many of whom have serious illnesses.

The second place not to buy a puppy is from a puppy farm over the Internet. Always buy from a breeder. The trouble is that it can be hard to tell if a website belongs to a breeder or a puppy farm.

Always buy your pet from a breeder

Checklist: Breeders vs. Puppy Farms

Does this website belong to a breeder? Check:

✔ That they are selling only one or two types of dogs. (Puppy farms will be selling a number of different breeds.)

✔ That they are involved in other dog-related activities such as education or showing. (Puppy farms are only concerned with selling puppies.)

✔ That they are concerned about who you are and whether you are suited to having one of their dogs. (Puppy farms only want to make money.)

✔ By visiting the premises if it is feasible. (Puppy farms will not let you look around.)

Costs

Guess how much the average pet will cost you over its lifetime? $5,000? $10,000? Think again.

Approximate costs for pets at the time of publication, include the following:

- Purchasing the animal (ranging from about $25 to over $3,000)
- Neutering (up to $275 for dogs and $220 for cats)
- Immunizations (an annual fee of about $160 for cats and $240 for dogs)
- Annual registration (about $10 per year — a neutered/spayed animal is slightly cheaper than an intact one)
- Clipping (from $40, several times a year)
- And if you or your house aren't up to it, bathing ($25)

So what does this add up to?

Lifetime* Cost of Owning a Pet		
	Annual Cost	**Lifetime Cost**
Purchase		$ 500
Neutering		$ 275
Puppy School		$ 250
Microchipping		$ 80
Immunization	$240	$2,400
Deworming	$ 100	$ 1,000
Registration	$ 10	$ 100
Clipping	$ 120	$ 1,200
Bathing	$ 300	$ 3,000
Veterinary Fees		$ 2,500
Kennel Costs	$ 500	$ 5,000
Food	$ 75	$ 7,500
Toys/Leads	$ 50	$ 500
Beds		$ 200
	TOTAL	**$24,505**

*Assuming the pet lives for the average 10 years

If you think this is unreasonable, it's not! *The Bankwest Family Pooch Index*[39] agrees that the cost of owning a dog for its lifespan will be more than $20,000, with Gen Y as a group spending more than any other group on their pets.

What else do cats and dogs need?

Apart from the collar, tag, leash, and toys, you'll need to think about a bed of some sort and a car restraint or carry box.

Cats will need litterboxes. The general rule is that you need one litterbox per cat plus one extra, which means that two cats require three litterboxes. This is because cats can be quite fussy and think that a used litterbox is like a dirty public toilet.

You will also need to think about storage space for food. Animal food is significantly cheaper to buy in bulk, but do you have the room to store a 30-pound bag of dog food?

Food

You can choose either wet or dry food, but make sure it is balanced. It will say so on the label, or you can ask your vet.

When considering which food to use, remember that dry food has many (mainly waste-related) advantages. Dry food usually results in less feces, and the feces itself is less smelly. That's got to be a good thing.

> **Dry food has many (mainly waste-related) advantages**

The poop is also firmer, so it is easier to remove from the litterbox or pick up in a plastic poop bag. And finally, because the food is more nutritionally dense, the volumes of food required are smaller, and so it is easier to carry the food home and to store once you get there.

Premium or economy food?

Just as in a human's diet, with pets, there is healthy everyday food and not-so-healthy occasional food.

While you can treat your pet with cheap generic brand pet snacks, with everyday food, you should aim to go for a premium brand. Premium brands are more expensive than generic brands. While it may not seem a wise economic decision, it probably is. You will buy premium food less often because you feed your pet less of it each day due to its high nutritional density.

You will also be sure that you are doing the right thing nutritionally by your pet, and as a result, they may suffer less from dietary upsets.

Daily feeding routine

Up to the age of six months, you should feed cats and dogs three times per day. This does not necessarily mean at breakfast, lunch, and dinner time but ideally would be at intervals of about eight hours apart (say 8 a.m., 5:30 p.m., and 11 p.m.). Some cats may be good at grazing, in which case you can leave food in their bowl for them to eat throughout the day. Most dogs are not good grazers, and however much you put into their bowl, it will be gone in two minutes.

After six months, you can revert to twice a day feeding. Always make sure you have fresh, clean water available at all times.

One thing - do not feed cats dog food. Yes, it's tempting because often it is cheaper, but it is too low in protein and fat and does not contain Taurine, an amino acid that cats are unable to produce themselves. If fed exclusively on dog food, cats can end up with heart problems.

Do not feed cats dog food

Dog Waste

How do you feel about poop? You'll need to get used to dealing with it if you have a pet. You can be fined or imprisoned for not doing so. (I'm not kidding – in New York City it's $250 if you break the "pooper scooper law" or up to 10 days' imprisonment![40])

So how do you do it? For dogs, using a dog waste bag, turn the bag inside out, put your hand in it, then pick up the waste and turn the bag back out the right way out. Voila! Poop on the inside and hand (hopefully clean) on the outside. Tie it up and throw it into a trash can.

Most parks have free bags, or you can buy a roll of them from the pet store. Be warned: biodegradable ones make you feel good but sometimes split with less than appealing results.

With cats, if you use a clumping litter, it is easy to extract the waste as it forms discreet lumps. Use the same technique to remove it as per the dog waste bag as above.

Keeping Your Pet Healthy

The following is advice from a vet, but please note that the circumstances of your own pet may differ, so consult your local practice for specific information.

Immunizations for cats

Immunizations for cats from a vaccinated mother are required at about eight weeks, at 12 weeks, at 16 weeks, and then annually. In some circumstances, immunizations are only required every three years after the initial kitten vaccinations.

If the kitten is a stray, it is assumed that the mother was not vaccinated (and so there has been no immunity passed on), so immunizations in this case may be started as early as two weeks.

Outdoor cats also need treatment for FIV (similar to HIV), a virus that can lead to feline AIDS, so this will be given at 12 and 16 weeks with a booster required every one, two or three years, depending on the recommendations from the vaccine manufacturer.

It should be noted that the rabies vaccine needs to be given to all cats and dogs at 12 weeks with a booster required every one, two or three years, again depending on the recommendations from the vaccine manufacturer. You will be required to have a certificate stating that your animal has received their rabies shots.

Immunizations for dogs

Immunizations for dogs are also required at about eight weeks, at 12 weeks, at 16 weeks, and then annually. In some circumstances, immunizations are only required every three years after the initial puppy vaccinations.

Again, if the puppy is a stray, it is assumed that the mother was not vaccinated (and so there has been no immunity passed on), so immunizations in this case may be started as early as two weeks.

Rabies shots will be given at 12 weeks with a booster required every one, two or three years, depending on the recommendations from the vaccine manufacturer.

Worms

All pets also need a regular annual intestinal deworming treatment (there are many effective anti-parasitic medications, including Milbemax for cats or Drontal for dogs). And all dogs also need heartworm treatment.

Fleas

When it comes to fleas, the case is not so clear cut. Some people are horrified by fleas and will always treat their pets, even if the pets do not go outside. Some people will only treat for fleas over summer, when fleas are more prevalent. And some people will only treat when there is an indication that their pet has fleas, such as when they scratch and lick themselves more than normal or when you can see the fleas by separating the fur and looking closely.

To treat fleas, there are both pills and topical treatments

To treat fleas, there are both pills and topical treatments. These can treat just for fleas alone or treat for fleas plus intestinal worms and/or heartworms. One reason to keep fleas under control (apart from keeping them out of your carpets!) is that an animal's skin can become sensitized if they are repeatedly bitten, and they may develop an allergy to the saliva in the flea's bite. If this occurs, the ensuing skin condition will have to be treated over the long term, maybe for the rest of the pet's life.

Common Cat Complaints

The things that might concern your cat or that will make you take Tiger to see the vet can include:

Hairballs

Cats groom themselves and, as a result, can ingest their own fur. Occasionally this may be vomited up as a tube of matted, slimy hair. Think Puss in Boots in *Shrek 2* and you'll get an idea why this is best avoided for both you and your cat. Grooming your cat often and feeding it a special hairball food can help.

Fight wounds

Cats can suffer from fight wounds when they are out and about, which is one of several good reasons to stop them from roaming the streets at night. Depending on the wounds, the cat might require antibiotics or surgery.

Locking them in at night will also stop them from being hit by a car or hunting then eating small native animals which in most cases is not good for either your cat or the native animal!

Respiratory tract infections

Like us, cats can get colds with symptoms such as a cough, a runny nose and eyes, and mouth ulcers. Generally, these infections are viral, and your main job is to keep the cat well hydrated and comfortable.

Bad teeth

Cats' teeth are hard to clean with a toothbrush (no, I'm not joking, you can get cat toothbrushes), so to avoid bad teeth, you can try a couple of things. Give them raw chicken bones to crunch on, or try specific foods for tooth care that have larger kibble and are less brittle. This allows the tooth to be inserted farther into each piece and therefore cleans it as the cat eats.

Being hit by a car

I'm not sure I need to say anything here. Try to keep your cat in at night; it's just sensible.

Arthritis

Like humans, cats suffer from age-related, degenerative (wearing down) arthritis that causes them pain, stiffness, and disfiguration. It can make them grumpy too. Treat this with weight loss, physical therapy, and drugs such as corticosteroids and painkillers.

Poisoning

Many household items and plants are toxic to cats — please see the list further on in this chapter.

Many household items and plants are toxic to dogs and cats

Common Dog Complaints

Cuts from running into things

Dogs get lacerations from running into things — like the sharp edges of a piece of furniture or a park bench. These can need stitches and/or antibiotics.

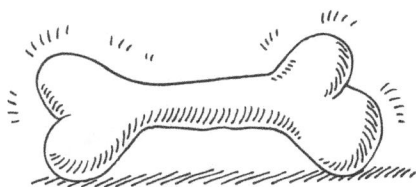

Being hit by a car

All dogs should be kept on a leash except in leash-free areas. Even if you are just crossing the road to chat with a friend, always put your dog on a leash. Your dog may be extremely well trained but can still be distracted by a cat or a particularly interesting dog on the other side of the road.

Gastroenteritis

Dogs are scavengers and often get gastroenteritis from scavenging when out and about (Cat poo! Dead animals! Leftover sandwiches!) or from eating too much of a good thing. Treatment involves keeping the pet well hydrated and reintroducing bland food such as boiled rice and steamed chicken in small doses. In a worst case scenario, your vet may give an injection to stop vomiting and insert a drip to keep your pet hydrated.

Kennel or Canine Cough

While dogs get fewer respiratory infections than cats, they can get the highly infectious Kennel Cough (also known as Canine Cough). The dog will have a persistent and strong cough but will generally still be able to eat his food. This will normally resolve by itself, although your vet may give your pet antibiotics.

Arthritis

Dogs can also suffer from age-related arthritis due to the wearing down of their joints. This can be very painful, making them stiff and grumpy. Treatment can involve painkillers, corticosteroids, physical therapy, and weight loss.

Keeping Your Pet Safe

There are a number of common household items and plants that are toxic to cats and dogs, so be careful if you have these around the house.

Household items that are toxic to your animals

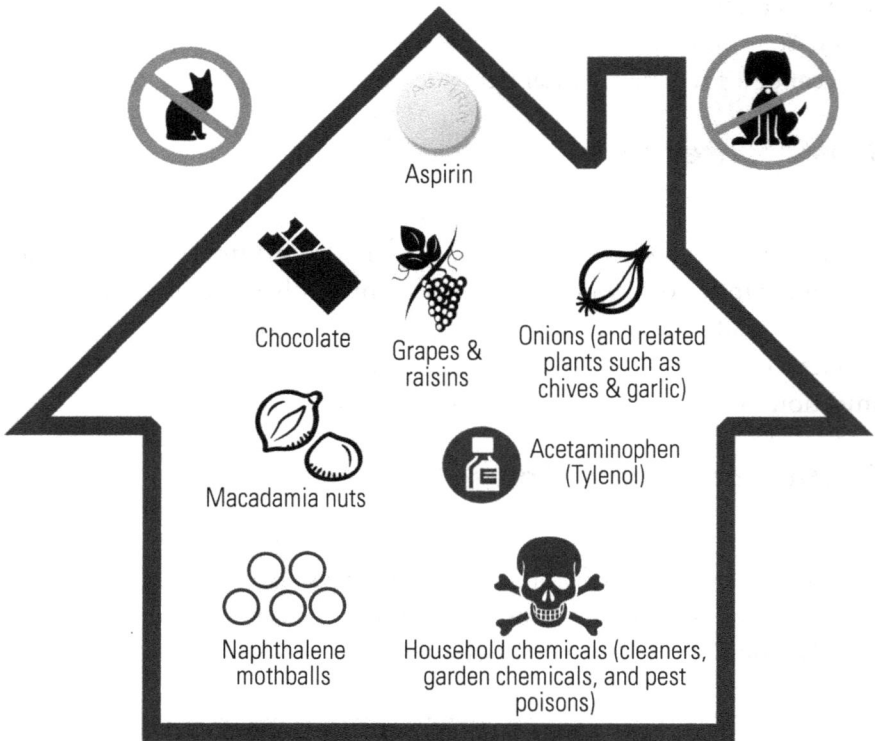

Aspirin

Chocolate

Grapes & raisins

Onions (and related plants such as chives & garlic)

Macadamia nuts

Acetaminophen (Tylenol)

Naphthalene mothballs

Household chemicals (cleaners, garden chemicals, and pest poisons)

Item	Details	Dogs	Cats
Aspirin	Even just one pill	Toxic	Toxic
Chocolate	Contains Theobromine, which can cause seizures and may result in death. Dark chocolate is worse than white. Cats don't like chocolate so less of a risk for them.	Toxic	Toxic
Grapes & raisins	May lead to kidney failure	Toxic	
Onions (and related plants such as chives & garlic)	Can damage red blood cells, leading to anaemia and also gastrointestinal problems	Toxic	Toxic
Macadamia nuts		Toxic	
Acetaminophen (Tylenol)	Can cause anemia and ulcers and can lead to kidney and liver failure	Toxic	Toxic
Naphthalene mothballs	May kill pets (and they're not too great for us either)	Toxic	Toxic
Household chemicals (cleaners, garden chemicals, and pest poisons)		Toxic	Toxic

Plants that are toxic to animals

Lilies are very toxic to cats (even the pollen) and slightly less toxic to dogs. They may cause heart problems, possibly resulting in death. Cyclamens are also toxic to both cats and dogs and can cause vomiting and diarrhea.

Jade plants can cause vomiting, depression, a slowing heart rate, and unconsciousness, and corn, philodendrons, aloe, and elephant's ear are all toxic to both dogs and cats.

Should I call the vet?

You wake up and your pet is behaving weirdly. She's listless and not eating her food. Should you go to the vet?

My advice is to develop a relationship with your local vet <u>before</u> your pet becomes ill. Visit the clinic, and get to know the staff. Then, when you need advice, you can give the clinic a call. You probably won't get to speak to the vet right away, but the nurses are very good at phone triage and can tell you if what you have is an emergency or if it's more of a "wait and see" type problem.

Being responsible

Be a responsible pet owner by always doing the following:

✔ Keep your dog on a leash unless it is in an off-leash area.

✔ Microchip and register both cats and dogs.

✔ Keep cats inside overnight to protect them from fighting and from cars and also to keep them from hunting native animals.

✔ Enroll your puppy in classes for socialization.

24-hour emergency centers

There are lots of 24-hour emergency centers, and you should try to find one that is close to your home. Check with your usual clinic to see if they have a relationship with one or if there is one that they particularly recommend. Be warned that some emergency clinics might offer a more comprehensive service than the situation warrants or than you are used to. You can end up spending a fortune.

Pet insurance

Your vet would most likely recommend pet insurance, particularly for the most expensive events that may occur. It can be only a couple of dollars a week for peace of mind. Make sure you look at the deductible that will be charged (this is the amount you yourself must pay when you make a claim, before payment from the insurance company kicks in). Also check for breeds that may be excluded from a policy and exclusions that are related to the age of your pet.

Give your own health fund or household insurer a call to see if they have pet insurance. This can make the whole business cheaper.

Neutering Your Pet

Neutered pets are more affectionate and less dominant

And now a word on the neutering of pets. Whether you call it castration, spaying, fixing, or getting snipped, your vet would recommend it for animals that are not going to be used for showing or breeding. There are a number of reasons why this is a good thing and these include your pet becoming more affectionate, less dominant and not coming in to heat.

Why you should neuter your pets

- Neutering tends to make both males and females less dominant, aggressive, and prone to wandering.

- Your pets may become more affectionate, and your pets can't get cancer or infections of the reproductive organs.

- You avoid the mess of females going into heat and potentially the arrival of kittens or puppies.

- Registration is (slightly) cheaper for a neutered pet.

- And here's a big one: It will stop the marking of territory. That's when your pet pees around the place to show that it's the boss. Yuck.

What to Do If You Go Away

Cats

Cats can be happily left in the house while you go away for up to a week as long as someone can come in twice a day. The morning visit is to feed and water them, to clean up the kitty litter, and to let them out for the day. The night-time visit is to feed and water them again and to lock them in for the night.

If you are away for more than a week, cats will become stressed, so you must either put them into a cattery (at the time of writing, up to $55 a day) or arrange for someone to housesit. Cats are not particularly happy to move into someone else's house for a short period of time or to go on vacation with you, as they are generally very attached to their houses and moving can be disturbing for them.

Dogs

Dogs are not happily left alone for any period of time at all. You will need to take them with you, re-house them with someone familiar (make sure they can't escape), have someone housesit to look after them, or put them into a kennel. This can cost up to a whopping $85 a day.

Dogs need to be immunized against Kennel Cough to stay at a boarding facility even though this is not considered a core vaccine.

How to find a good kennel

Your vet clinic may offer a pet-sitting service, and they may also be able to recommend a good cattery or kennel. Pet-owning friends can offer good advice, but be warned that many catteries and kennels are situated in rural areas and if you are not, this may involve a long drive or a costly pick-up and delivery service. If possible, you should organize a visit to meet the staff and look at the facilities, and make sure that you test the kennel or cattery for a weekend stay before you plan a longer one.

Bear in mind that your pet might never want to come home! Some facilities offer massage, private televisions, individual playtimes, pet brushings, and more…at a price.

So that's it. I hope that you and your pet have a long and happy life together.

Five Top Tips

1. Buy your pets from a pet breeder or shelter. Don't ever look for pets in a pet store or online — they're likely to be from a puppy farm.

2. Dry food will result in dog waste that is smaller, dryer, and less smelly. Go dry!

3. Don't feed cats dog food as it can result in them having heart problems.

4. Generally, dogs and cats need to be immunized at 8, 12, and 16 weeks with boosters annually. This will include a rabies vaccine, and they will need a certificate to prove they have had it.

5. Get your pet neutered. Registration may be slightly cheaper for neutered animals, and your pet will most likely be less dominant and more affectionate.

With many thanks to Dr. Mike Hutchinson, Pittsburgh, Pennsylvania, and Dr. Donald Ward, Melbourne, Victoria for their help in writing this chapter.

CHAPTER 11

Things with Leaves and Stems

Your room's a mess. Your love life's a disaster. Your grades are appalling. And you're not even sure the family cat likes you anymore. Never fear! A cheerful plant or bunch of flowers can make everything seem all right.

Haven't Got Time to Read the Whole Chapter? Read This.

1. The best place to buy fresh flowers is at a market where turnover is high; the worst is from a roadside seller where the flowers can be affected by wind, light, and pollution.

2. Modern fake flowers are surprisingly lovely, and you can mix them with a smaller bunch of fresh flowers for an impressive display at little ongoing cost.

3. Tropical plants make a good choice to have inside as they enjoy a warmer temperature.

4. Generally, smaller household plants will need to be re-potted every year, with larger ones needing to be done every two years.

5. The easiest herbs to grow are the perennial ones — once planted (and looked after!), they will keep on growing for years. Parsley, thyme, rosemary, and mint are all good choices.

Buying Flowers

Your choice of flower will determine how long you have them — some will last for weeks, and others will be here and gone in a couple of days. Choose carefully, particularly if you have a limited budget.

Longest lasting flowers

The longest lasting flowers (although they can be tricky to find) are those that grow in arid areas, such as everlasting daisies (e.g., paper daisy) and statice. They can be very colorful, will last for several weeks in your vase, and if you hang them upside down to dry first, they can last for years. Can't beat that.

Lilies can last for up to two weeks

Orchids, lilies, chrysanthemums, and carnations are also a good choice. Lilies can last for up to two weeks if you get them when they are tightly budded. Similarly, Alstroemeria (Peruvian Lilies) last extremely well, are very cheap, and come in a huge range of colors. Don't buy them if you have cats, as all lilies are extremely toxic to your feline friends.

Orchids, lilies, chrysanthemums, and carnations are all generally easily available, are budget friendly, and, even better, if they are white, you can stick them in water colored with food dye and they will change color. Cool — a living science experiment!

Enjoy, but don't get too attached

Roses are probably the best known of all flowers, and you can buy them everywhere — from the gas station to the high-end florist. They come in a huge range of colors and varieties and can be reasonably priced. Gerberas, too, are widely available and are also quite inexpensive. These two types of flowers are good solid investments as long as they are fresh and should see out a week on your kitchen counter.

Forget it

Tulips and irises are for the rich or insane. Don't be tempted by them. Those beautiful tulips are exquisite, but in a day or so, you will see them dropping their petals onto the table. The same with irises — they will break your heart.

Air cleaning plants & flowers

If you are looking to keep the air inside your place clean, some plants act as air purifiers, and these include chrysanthemums, peace lilies, English ivy, bamboo palm, and gerberas.

Where to buy them

The best place to buy flowers is at a market — some wholesale sellers are willing to sell to individuals as long as you don't resell the flowers yourself. The next best place is a florist, and you should be very happy if they are presented in glass containers (black plastic buckets hide a multitude of sins). The worst place to buy them is from a street seller with buckets on the side of the road or any location that is exposed to light, wind, or pollution.

flowers at the grocery store can be a good buy

Surprisingly, flowers at the grocery store can be a good buy. They are invariably cheap, and if you find out what day they regularly come in and buy them on that day, they can be very fresh. Don't buy ones that have been marked down — they're *cheap* because they're one step off *dead*.

What to look for when buying flowers

Although this can be hard to see if the flowers are in black plastic buckets, look for clean water and tightly budded flowers. Taking a surreptitious sniff of the water can make you seem very weird but will tell you as much as looking at them. Leaves should be firm with no browning on the edges.

Ideally, you want to buy flowers from a store that has a high turnover, so go for one that is popular, with lots of pedestrian traffic. If you can, find out when your local flower seller gets their fresh flowers in. It will not be every day, and if you coincide your buying with the day the florist goes to the market, you should have longer lasting flowers at your place.

Case Study:
Know Your Flowers

It was the day before Valentine's Day, and Zach wanted to be prepared for the next day, when he was meeting his girlfriend, Hannah, for breakfast. He stopped at a roadside flower seller on the way home from work to buy some flowers. He knew how much she loved tulips, so he gulped, forked over $50, and bought two small bunches of them. He took them home and put them in a vase ready to give to her the next morning. When he woke up on Valentine's Day, there were tulip heads around the base of the vase, and those stems that were still intact were bent over kissing the countertop. There was no way he could give them to her now.

Lesson: Know which flowers to buy, and be careful where you buy them.

Fake flowers

Are you thinking retirement community entrance hall or doctor's office? Don't! There are some really beautiful fake flowers on the market, such as lilies, magnolias, and peonies, and you'll need to touch them to tell them apart from their genuine floral sisters. But be warned — they are horribly expensive! Save up for them, then mix them with a smaller bunch of fresh flowers for an impressive display at a reasonable ongoing cost.

Keeping Flowers

Transporting flowers

If you are transporting flowers any distance, make sure they have a wet paper towel wrapped around the end of the stems, covered by a plastic bag securely tied on to avoid drips. Keep them out of the heat and sun, ideally in a slightly cool temperature. Make sure that they are adequately supported, not rolling around in the back of your car! And put them in water as soon as you can.

Help! My flowers haven't opened!

So you've bought a great bunch of flowers to have on display at your dinner party tonight. Trouble is the flowers are all shut and the arrangement looks like a bunch of sticks in a vase.

To overcome this, you can try a few things: put warm (not hot) water in the vase, gently pull the buds apart at the tip (only do this if the bud has started to open; otherwise, you'll end up pulling them to pieces), or blow on them. Yep, blow on them! These methods won't always work, but you've got the best chance with roses and lilies.

How to make them last

To make flowers last, try the following:

- If you are lucky enough to be picking flowers from your own back yard, pick them in the early morning or late afternoon. They'll be much fresher and will last longer. Always cut the stems on a slant and with pruning shears as this gives a clean cut and the greatest surface area from which the flower can absorb water.

- If you are buying flowers, when you get them home, cut off their stems at an angle with pruning shears, removing about one inch from the bottom. Try not to use a knife — you'll wreck both the flowers AND the knife.

- If the flower has a woody stem, remove the outer wood about three inches from the end of the stalk to allow water to be absorbed.

- Remove any leaves that will end up below the water line. They'll quickly turn rank, and the water will smell disgusting.

- Immediately put them in clean water with added sugar or Sprite (to provide nourishment) and either a splash of white vinegar, bleach, or vodka (which all reduce bacterial growth). Don't overdose as you'll end up with dead flowers (or at least drunk ones).

- Alternatively, you can add an aspirin to the water (½ an aspirin if it's a small vase).

- Ideally, you should change the flower water each day, cutting the stems again and washing out the vase with hot soapy water to remove all bacteria. Realistically, if you can do this every couple of days and just top up the water in between, you'll be half way there.

Change the flower water each day

- Make sure that the water covers the shortest stem in the bunch — usually ¾ of the way up the vase is a good choice.

How else do I keep them fresh?

Keep them out of drafts and away from heat sources such as direct sunlight or heaters. At night, put them into the coolest room of the house (often the bathroom) or outside but not in the refrigerator. Heat will cause the flowers to open too quickly, and this is what we are trying to avoid.

Displaying Flowers

What vases do I need?

Personally, I never seem to have exactly the right vase to display my flowers — they're always too short, too fat, too narrow, too tall. But remember, you can use almost any container, and repetition can be the key to a beautiful arrangement. Try an odd number (yep, weird, but looks better odd) of the same type of jelly jar with a flower in each. Or perhaps an old pitcher, pewter mug, or even a fishbowl.

If you are sticking to real vases, go for clear glass ones. At a minimum, you will need:

- A small, narrow 4-inch vase for a single flower.
- A tall, large vase for an arrangement of flowers such as lilies.
- A couple of medium-sized low vases for bouquets.

Checklist: How do I clean a vase?

Hot soapy water with a bottlebrush is ideal, but for stubborn stains, take your pick of the following:

✔ Try a denture cleanser tablet dissolved in water. You can buy these in a box quite cheaply at the grocery store, and they work great. (And for you multi-taskers out there, they're also great for those brown stains in coffee cups — as well as for your false teeth.)

✔ Add a teaspoon of baking soda to some warm water in a vase. Add vinegar till it fizzes; then shake and rinse.

✔ Sprinkle dishwashing powder into the vase, and then add a little water. Shake it all about (doing the Hokey-Pokey if you want) and rinse.

How to make a small bouquet

Start with your feature flower or, if you don't have one, your foliage. Holding the bouquet, spin it around, sliding in your other flowers and foliage, starting with the largest and moving to the smallest and trying to keep it even from all angles. Generally, you should have an odd number of your feature flowers, say five or seven.

Tie the bouquet up with either string (which florists would advise) or rubber bands (which are easy and practical). When you are finished, the stems below your tying point should be in the shape of a clown's hat, and the bouquet should be able to stand up on the counter by itself. If you are giving it away, tell the recipient not to take off the rubber band as it will collapse and lose its shape.

How to do a simple vase arrangement

Place your foliage in the vase, and then individually insert your focal flowers. These should be evenly spaced, say in the shape of a diamond (four flowers) plus one flower in the middle. The total number of focal flowers should be an odd number.

Add in the other flowers you have chosen so that size and color are balanced when looking at the arrangement from the front.

How to wrap flowers in paper

First fold your paper in half but slightly askew so the edges don't match. Lay your bouquet down with the flowers almost reaching the unfolded edges and the stems towards the fold. Roll the bouquet along the counter. Finally, secure with tape down the edge and a ribbon or raffia around the waist of the bouquet.

Indoor Plants

Instead of flowers, you can always go for an indoor plant. Flowering tropical plants make a good choice to have inside as they enjoy a warmer temperature. Phaelenopsis orchids (those ones on the long, tall stem) last forever if you treat them well and don't overwater them, and cyclamens will grace your house for months on end, especially if you put them outside at night. (When they die, throw them outside somewhere in their pots and forget them. Lo and behold! In a year's time they will surprise you with more flowers.)

Jade plants (Crassula Ovata), the succulents with the little squishy, round green leaves, will survive almost anywhere. This is just as well because according to some people, they indicate your future wealth status – the more abundant the plant, the more abundant your wealth! In particular, they love full sunlight, and a good trim will make them bushier. Don't over water. You can replant any offcuts after leaving them for a week to harden, thereby making lots of little jade plants (and lots more money!).

White Anthurium love a temperature of about 70°F and will thrive in a bathroom while needing little care and surviving massive neglect.

Checklist: Caring for indoor plants

✔ Read the little care tag that came with your plant – you can pretty safely assume that the person who grew it knows how to look after it.

✔ Make sure they get enough light.

✔ Water only as instructed, enough so that the leaves don't go brown and fall off but not too much to drown it.

✔ Talking about leaves going brown – cut them off! If you've been distracted and there are lots of dead leaves, the plant might look bald, but with some luck, it will recover.

✔ If the leaves are yellow, it can be a sign of too much water.

✔ Don't let the plant get wet feet. Make sure there are holes in the bottom of the pot. If it's a decorative one with no holes, grab a drill and a ceramic drill bit and put some in.

✔ Look out for pests (on your plants I mean).

✔ Make sure you avoid any plants that are toxic to your animals.

✔ And finally, don't despair if you lose a plant or two – see it as an opportunity to try out something new.

Repotting plants

If you are successful in not killing your potted plants, at some stage, they will need to be repotted into a larger pot so that their roots do not become cramped. You can tell if a plant needs repotting if it stops growing or if you can see roots poking out through the drainage holes or up through the soil. Generally, smaller household plants will need to be repotted every year, with larger ones needing to be done every two years.

Here's how to do it, even if you can't reliably tell a stem from a root:

1. The day before, give the pot a good watering. It's going to be an easier project if the soil is moist.

2. Turn the pot upside down, and putting your fingers around the stem, give it a good shake. If the plant doesn't come out of the pot, give it a bang against the edge of a table. Be gentle — you don't want to break the pot, the plant, OR the table!

3. Once you have the plant out of the pot and upside down in your hands, tickle the roots, loosening them up. You will lose some soil, but that's okay.

4. If they are very tightly coiled, give the roots a trim.

5. Put some potting mix in the bottom of your new pot, enough so that when you put in the plant, it will be sitting at about the right level in the pot.

6. Place the plant in, and then put potting mix all around, gently pushing it down. Continue until you have potting mix up to about an inch below the top of the pot

7. Give the pot a drink, and pat yourself on the back. Don't fertilize the pot for a month. Good job!

And a Final Word on Herbs

However small your backyard or patio, or even if you don't have one at all, you can still grow a few herbs. The easiest ones to grow are the perennial ones — once planted, they will keep on growing over a number of years. Parsley, thyme, rosemary, and mint are all good choices, but make sure that you put your mint in a pot, not a garden bed, or else it will take over everything in its path.

If you are lucky, basil will come back year after year in a garden bed, but once cilantro dies down, it's history, and you'll need to buy more.

Five Top Tips

1. For fresh flowers that last for ages, choose orchids, lilies, chrysanthemums, or carnations.

2. Read the little care tag that came with your plant — you can pretty safely assume that the person who grew it knows how to look after it.

3. Clean a stained vase with hot, soapy water and a bottle brush; for really stubborn stains, try a denture cleanser tablet. (Steal it from your grandma!)

4. To do a simple vase arrangement, insert your foliage, and then insert an odd number of focal flowers.

5. To get a bud to open more quickly, put the flowers in warm water and pull apart the buds at the tip.

CHAPTER 12

Other Things Mom's Been Trying to Tell You

Haven't Got Time to Read the Whole Chapter? Read This.

1. You will be judged by the way you behave. Stand out by being on time, writing thank you letters (or at least emails or texts), and being formal with older people.

2. First impressions count. Make sure you look people in the eyes, have a firm handshake, remember names, and show interest in other people.

3. When you are with others, leave your phone alone and in your pocket or bag. Show your companion that they are more important than your phone — even if you actually prefer your phone.

4. Don't use capitals in your online communications. IT'S RUDE AND SCARY.

5. When a relationship breaks up, don't expect that you will continue to be friends. Leave the other person in peace, don't call them when you've had one drink too many, and don't even think about break-up sex.

Etiquette

This chapter is about modern manners. You might think that etiquette is just a weird set of rules from a bygone era. Well, in a way, you're right, but it's really all about being considerate of people's needs and feelings and behaving in a way that shows respect for others.

People will make judgments about you based on the way you behave. Want to stand out from the crowd (but in a good way)? Try these.

Be on time

If you arrange to meet someone in a public place (such as a café or park), be there on time. Your friend will feel like an idiot hanging around by themselves, so don't be late. On the other hand, if you are going to someone's house, don't arrive right on time – give them 10 to 15 minutes; otherwise, you might find your host or hostess in their underwear.

Be formal with older people

Be formal when you meet much older people socially for the first time – call them Mr. or Mrs. It might feel strange or make you feel like a suck-up, but it will highlight you as being respectful and polite. (And they will usually ask you to call them by their first name anyway, so there's no great loss). Don't do this at the office – it would just be weird.

Thank you letters

Isn't it a great feeling to get a handwritten letter in your mailbox? Whenever you can, write one. People love them. The letter itself doesn't need to be too flashy, but try to make it sincere, and if it's a thank you, mention something about why you enjoyed the event or gift.

Having said that, it is also fine to send a thank you letter in the same format as you received the invitation. So if you are invited to an event on Facebook, then you can say thank you the same way; if you are invited by text, it's fine to send a thank you by text. Try to do it within a couple of days of the event, although if you forget, it's better late than never.

Meeting People

Generally

Making a good impression can happen right from the very first time you meet someone. You should try to:

Look people in the eye when talking to them

- Have a firm handshake — not a bone-breaker but also not one like a pathetic wet fish. The former says you are trying too hard; the latter is just off-putting.

- Look people in the eye when you are talking to them. Don't be weird about it, don't invade their personal space, and don't zoom in on them with radar eyes, but some eye contact is a good thing.

- Try to speak up, and don't mumble. It's annoying if people have to strain to hear you.

- Show interest in the other person. Ask them questions about themselves, and see if you have any common ground. You never know, you might both be interested in the local weavers of the Xinjiang Uyghur Autonomous Region.

- Try to remember and use their name. Some people use a mnemonic. For example, say you meet an exceptionally neat woman named Christine — think "Pristine Christine."

Tips for meeting the parents (uh oh)

It can be really nerve-wracking to meet the parents of your current favorite person for the first time. No doubt you want to make a good impression, so try the following.

Checklist: Meeting the parents for the first time

✔ Dress smartly — depending on your gender, don't wear clothes that are too revealing or too casual.

✔ Don't be late, and take a small gift such as a bottle of wine, if appropriate, or some chocolates.

✔ Turn off your cell phone before you go inside.

✔ Shake hands and make eye contact.

✔ Watch your table manners, and eat whatever is offered. Your partner should have warned the parents if you are unable to eat certain foods for medical, religious, or ethical reasons (such as meat, pork, or gluten). If there has been a slipup, accept the items on to your plate with no comment, and leave them on the side of the plate discreetly.

✔ Accept a modest second helping — this makes the cook feel that you really liked what they made.

✔ Drink only a modest amount of alcohol — things can go wrong in so many different ways if you don't.

✔ Show interest in younger siblings, pets, and any evident interests of the parents, and be careful discussing politics, sex, or religion.

Tips for Going Out

Replying to invitations

When you receive an invitation, try to reply to it as quickly as possible. You should reply in the same way in which you received the invitation. So if it's on Facebook, then reply that way. If it's by SMS, reply by SMS. And if you receive a written invitation, you should reply in writing unless the invitation has an email address or phone number on it, in which case you can reply in either of these ways.

Avoid pulling out of parties on Facebook. I know it's standard behavior, but it's just not right. Don't accept then closer to the date pull out just because you don't feel like going anymore, because your friends aren't going, or because something better has come up. Think about the host. How bad will they feel having 100 people say they'll come to their party and then finding they're down to only 20 on the night of?

Bringing someone along

Unless you have a "+1" on Facebook or your invitation says "& friend," don't ask if you can bring someone along. Numbers at parties can be limited by finances or the size of the venue, and it can embarrass the host to ask.

Being in control

When you go out, try not to misbehave! There's nothing worse than waking up the next morning and remembering what you

Try not to misbehave!

did — or, even worse, not remembering what you did. Besides the obvious humiliation, you put yourself at risk in all sorts of ways, so don't drink or take other substances that cause you to lose control and embarrass yourself. Wait till you get home before you go wild.

Be inclusive

So you're at a dinner and seated next to the man or woman of your dreams on one side and a real bore on the other. Be a good guest! Talk to them both for about equal amounts of time.

It's all just about being considerate. You will appreciate how good this advice is when you are next seated between two people who both turn their backs on you and talk to others all night.

Going to two parties on one night

Don't go to two or more parties on one night — it's not fair to the host who has tried hard to put on a good party and who is hoping it will be a great night. There's nothing worse than seeing half your guests disappear after an hour or so.

And which one should you choose? It's the one you were invited to first. If both invitations arrive about the same time, then you have the luxury of choosing the one you'd rather be at.

Going to Someone's House

Take a gift

When you visit someone's house, take a small gift. It doesn't need to be too flashy and can be something simple or, even better, something homemade or homegrown. Try a jar of jam or chutney, a small bunch of flowers from your back yard, or a small container of homemade cookies.

If you hear that someone is unwell, why not deliver some food to their house so they don't have to worry about cooking? A good thing to deliver is a quiche as this is easy to transport, can be eaten hot or cold, and lasts for several days if they already have other plans.

When it comes to birthdays, don't go overboard on the gifts as this will make your budget run off the rails. Again, why not give something homemade? This is more meaningful than something that you have just quickly bought on the way home from work.

Table manners

When you are at someone's house for dinner, don't start eating before the host has started. If they tell you to begin before them, then go ahead; otherwise, you should wait until they are seated and have started eating before you begin.

Send a thank you

As mentioned earlier, make sure you thank the host the next day. If you can't manage to put pen to paper, phone or Facebook is fine.

Hosting Guests at Your House

Seeing people at the door

When someone arrives at your house, make sure you greet them at the door. Don't call out "Come on in; the door's open." Going to the door makes guests feel welcome. You should also walk guests to the door when they are leaving. Yes, right to the very door. And to their car or cab if they are elderly. One other thing: Make sure your outdoor lights are on if it's dark when they arrive and when they leave.

Introductions

Practice making good introductions. Always say the name of the person you are showing the most respect to first (e.g., parents, grandparents, your girlfriend or boyfriend, or your boss) and repeat the names. For example, you would say

Practice making good introductions

"Grandma, I'd like you to meet my friend Andrew. Andrew, this is my grandma, Mrs. Smith." If introducing two people and you know you are going to have to leave them, it can be helpful to mention something that they have in common (e.g., "Jessica, I'd like you to meet Michael. Michael, this is Jessica. Did you know that you both play basketball?") Then they've got something to talk about when you disappear.

Setting the table

Glasses

The shorter stemmed glass with the biggest bowl is the red wine glass, the taller stemmed glass with the smaller bowl is for white wine, and the narrow, taller flute is for champagne. The glass without the stem is for water.

Wine glasses and a water glass should be placed directly north of the cutlery on the right-hand side of the setting.

Cutlery

By this stage, I'll take a wild guess that you can tell a fork from a knife and a spoon! In the case of a formal dinner, the only thing that might cause a problem is the bouillon spoon, which can either have a round bowl instead of an oval one or, in the case of a sterling silver setting, can be just a very large spoon (as large as a serving spoon).

Cutlery should be placed on each side of the plate in the order in which it will be used, starting at the outside. So on the right-hand side, you will have (starting on the outside) the bouillon spoon; the salad, appetizer, or fish knife (if you are having this course); the dinner knife; and then the dessert spoon. On the left-hand side, you will have (starting from the outside) the salad, appetizer, or fish fork; the dinner fork; and maybe a dessert fork.

You will have noticed that some people will place the dessert spoon and fork above the plate; this is perfectly acceptable.

Table decoration

Make sure your table decoration is not so high that it will obscure vision across the table. If it is, remove it before you sit down (which pretty much defeats its purpose, don't you think?).

Pepper & salt

Make sure that your pepper and salt shakers are full. These, as well as any mustards or sauces, should be removed before the dessert course is served.

Table seating

At a very formal dinner, the guest of honor (say the person whose birthday it is or an overseas visitor) should be seated on the right of the host or hostess of the opposite sex and will be served their meal first. The partner of the guest of honor will be seated at the right of the other host or hostess. So for instance, Will from overseas will be seated at the right of the hostess, and Will's partner Jenny (or maybe it's Matthew — doesn't matter) will be seated at the right of the host.

And...

Make sure the bathroom is tidy and the toilet is clean. Put away all your medications as that's no one's business but your own. There should be a clean hand-towel, and a small bunch of flowers would be nice.

Cell phone

There's a whole lot of etiquette around using your cell phone, but most of it relates to either not disturbing others or not being rude to the people you are with.

Checklist: Using your cell phone

When you are with others:

✔ If you are in the middle of something (such as arranging to go somewhere or sending an important text for work), try to finish it before you meet your friends.

✔ Turn your phone to silent, and put it away. Don't put your phone on the table unless it's been invited to dinner too.

✔ Give your full attention to your companion(s). Don't make a call, and let all voice calls go to voicemail.

✔ See if you can avoid checking Facebook, and don't read or write texts. The people you are with will be pleased that you think they are more interesting than someone on your phone.

✔ If you absolutely have to make a call or text someone, try to leave the table and do it in a discreet place. If that's just not possible, explain what you need to do to the people you are with. We've all got busy lives, so everyone understands that sometimes you just have to get on with it.

When you are in a public place:

✔ Don't shout into your cell phone. You don't need to! Your voice sounds softer to you on a cell phone than on a home phone. There's a whole lot of science to do with this, and if you're interested, read on, otherwise just skip this part. With a home phone, there is amplification of your voice into the earpiece (this is called Side Tone), but cell phones don't have it. This means your voice sounds louder to you on your home phone than on your mobile. Also, due to a thing called Automatic Gain Control, which cell phones do have, if you speak quietly, the signal is amplified, and if you speak loudly, it is diminished. For these two reasons, you need to consciously practice speaking quietly on a cell phone.[41]

✔ Be mindful of where you should avoid use of your phone completely (e.g., a library, a lecture, the theater, or in a place of religious worship).

✔ Never make store employees wait when while you finish a call. This is guaranteed to drive them mad and you'll have crazy bad service as a result.

✔ Try to avoid butt dials. Personally, I quite enjoy receiving them, but some people find them annoying, and they are potentially really embarrassing for you — imagine what terrible secrets you might reveal without even knowing it....

And lastly

✔ Never drive and use your cell phone. It's really, really stupid. As mentioned before, according to the National Safety Council, 1.6 million crashes are caused every year by using a cell phone while driving, including the death of 11 teenagers a day due to texting while driving.[42]

Keep your phone and yourself safe

✔ Make sure your phone regularly backs itself up. In particular, make sure you back up your photos, calendar, and address book.

✔ It's simple, but make sure you use a PIN to lock your phone.

✔ Keep your phone safe in your purse or pocket, and treat it as you would your wallet.

✔ Make a note of your phone's IMEI (International Mobile Equipment Identity) by dialing *#06#, looking on the back case if it's an iPhone, or looking under "settings" if it's an Android phone. Keep it somewhere other than stored on your phone... of course.

✔ Make sure you enter a contact for use in an emergency under "ICE" (in case of emergency) in your phone's address book, and if possible, put your blood type in the notes section. If you are involved in an accident, it can save precious time.

✔ Check your phone statement for unusual charges.

✔ Remember that if you don't pay your phone bill, it will affect your credit rating.

✔ And I've said it before but it's so important I'll say it again. Never, never, never use your cell phone while you are driving. Don't even glance at your phone to look at a text.

What do you do if your phone is stolen?

If your phone has been stolen, make sure you report it to your provider as soon as possible. You are responsible for any costs incurred on your phone until you do so. (For further details, read *What to do if you lose your phone* later in this book.)

Online Netiquette

And there are a few things to remember when you are online:

- Don't use capitals in your posts or emails. It's shouting, WHICH IS RUDE AND DISTURBING, NOT TO MENTION THREATENING.

- Be careful with your grammar and spelling. It says a lot about you. (And this is true in all your communications, not just electronic ones.)

- And have you ever received an email written at 3 a.m. and wondered what the person was doing up at that time? Be careful what time you are online because people will make judgments about you and your lifestyle.

- Don't forward jokes unless you are sure the recipient will appreciate them. Some people might not appreciate your humor (hard to believe); others might just not want the extra volume in their inbox.

- Tone is hard to judge online, so be careful with what you write. It can be easy for others to misinterpret what you have said.

- And on the other hand, be forgiving — perhaps what you understood is not what they meant.

- Don't write, post, or send something that you don't want everyone to read. If it's something cruel, are you that sort of person? And do you really want the person concerned to read it one day? Is it up to you to share that secret? And that photo — are you happy that it's starting a life out there on its own?

- Be careful about the photos you post on social media. Some companies ask for access to your page as part of the recruitment process, and that drunken photo of you under the table may not add to your employability.

- And while we're talking about photos, don't sext — it's out of your control once you've press send and it could float around the Internet for years. But of course you know that.

- If you are upset or the topic is controversial, wait a while and think before you post or send your thoughts on their way. If you're writing an email and planning to think about it before you send it, leave the To: box empty. That way it won't be sent by mistake.

- And finally, remember that there is always a person at the other end of your communications. Treat them with respect.

Relationships

Ending a relationship

If you need to end a relationship, don't send a text or do it on social media; be brave, and do it face to face. It's not going to be pretty, but once it's over, you can be happy that you did the honorable thing. Whatever has happened in the past, don't tell your partner what they've done wrong or list their faults, as tempting as that might seem. It's enough for you to say that the relationship is no longer working, that you wish them all the best, and that you hope you can still be friends. (Yep — everyone says that, and it's nice, but accept that in reality it probably won't happen; it's hard to stay friends with someone who's dumped you.)

Try to leave your ex-partner in peace, and avoid being there every step of the way in their grieving period. Treat them how you would hope to be treated in the same situation. And if you're the one who has been dumped, try to get on with your life, and avoid any drunk dialing. It's no good for anyone, and it's really bad for your self-esteem the next morning.

Break-up sex

No. No. No. Break-up sex is never a good idea as it can be confusing for both of you and may raise false expectations for the dumpee. Don't do it.

Break-up sex is never a good idea

Five Top Tips

1. Reply to invitations as soon as you can. You should reply by the same method in which you were invited.

2. It might be tempting, but don't go to two parties on one night — it's not fair to the host. You should always go to the party you were invited to first.

3. If you have to end a relationship, be brave and do it face to face.

4. Would you be happy for a future employer to look you up on social media? If not, clean it up and delete anything that might be offensive or give the wrong impression.

5. Don't sext — it's really risky. But of course you're smart enough to know that.

CHAPTER 13

OMG! It's An Emergency!

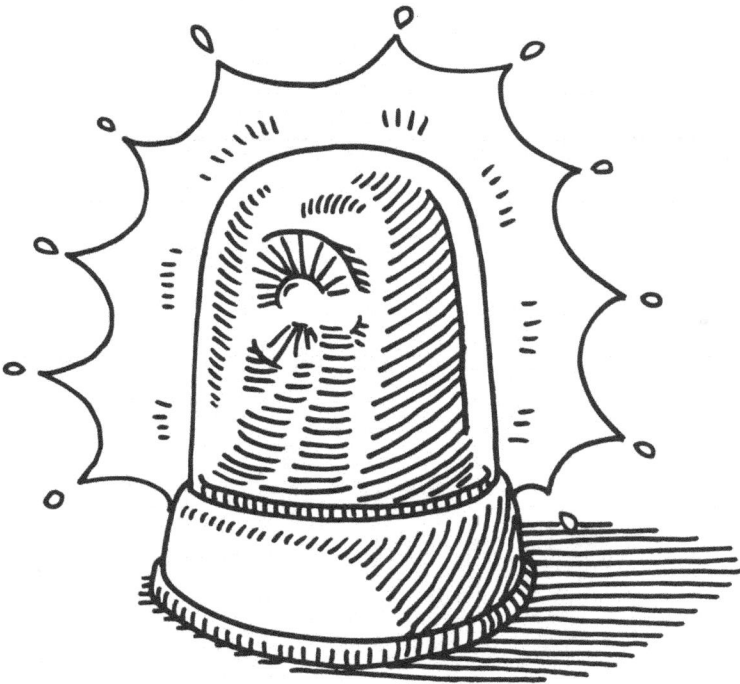

Haven't Got Time to Read the Whole Chapter? Read This.

1. Keep a photocopy or a photo on your cell phone of all your valuable information, including your cards and passport. Also keep a list of your property manager's preferred repairers on the fridge as well as their after hours emergency number.

2. If you lose your phone, have a good look for it then immediately notify your cell phone company to avoid any costs incurred by the person who's taken it.

3. If you need to dial 911, be prepared to say whether you need ambulance, police, or fire; make sure you know your address and the nearest cross-road; and don't hang up till they tell you to do so.

4. To put out a cooking fire, cover the pan with a lid or a fire blanket, and then turn off the burner if it is safe to do so.

5. If you live in an area where there are earthquakes or tornadoes, make sure you know how to turn off the gas valve in the house and where the closest safe-shelter is.

WHAT TO DO IN AN EMERGENCY

You all know that the emergency number in the U.S. is 911.

So life is cruising along smoothly; then out of the blue – disaster! Make sure you take a few basic steps beforehand so that if something bad happens, you can recover from it quickly. And try to stay calm and follow the advice in this chapter.

Checklist: Before an emergency

Make sure you gather all the following together and put them in a folder in a safe place, or at least store a version electronically:

✔ A copy of all your cards. This includes bank cards, your license, store cards, ID card, student cards, and travel cards.

✔ A copy of other important documents (e.g., your passport)

✔ Your cell phone's IMEI (15 digits) or MEID (drop the last digit of the IMEI to give 14 digits). There are several ways of getting them: try dialing *#06#, looking on the back of your iPhone, or going to "settings" on either your Android or iPhone.

✔ Important phone numbers (natural gas, electricity, water, home phone, property manager)

✔ If you are in a rental unit, a copy of the property manager's preferred repairers and their afterhours emergency phone number

✔ Photographs of any valuables such as electronics, jewelry, or decorative arts

✔ Receipts for purchases of insured items such as computers or TVs

You should also:

✔ Make sure you know how to turn the water off. There is often a lever outside, nearby the water meter or a faucet.

✔ It's important if you live in an area where there are earthquakes or tornadoes that you know how to turn off the gas valve in the house. You should also be aware of where the closest safe-shelter is.

✔ Find out where the circuit breaker box (for electricity) is.

✔ Install a "find my phone" app on your cell phone, such as *Find My iPhone* or *Wheres My Droid* (yep, there's no apostrophe in there).

✔ Test smoke alarms by pushing the little button with a broom handle once a month, and replace the battery once a year at a time you won't forget, such as the end of daylight saving time. If you are in a rental property, this should be done annually by the landlord or rental agency, but it's up to you to check in between times.

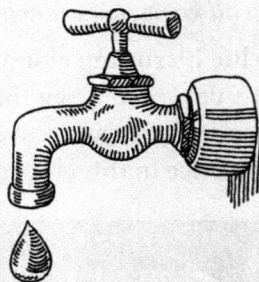

What to do if you have a car accident

1. Check that all passengers are okay. If not, call the emergency services.

2. Move your car out of the way of other traffic if it is safe to do so.

3. Get the details of the other driver, their car, and their insurance company (or take a photo of their license and the car's license plate).

4. If there are witnesses, get their contact details as well.

5. Take photos of any damage to either car.

6. File a police report — this can be important to claim on insurance.

7. Call your insurance company — they will arrange a tow truck if necessary.

8. Call to see if a friend can come and help without their own car. If your car is drivable, they can drive you and it home.

What to do if you lose your wallet

1. Look for it everywhere you've been (call around if you need to) as well as down the back of the couch, in bags, and in pockets.

2. Tell your friends and family you've lost your wallet, and ask them to look out for it.

3. Retrieve the copy of your cards, and start calling the banks to cancel and reissue them. Start with the ones that bear a financial risk (e.g., credit cards), and don't worry about ones like your library card. (No one's going to go wild with that!)

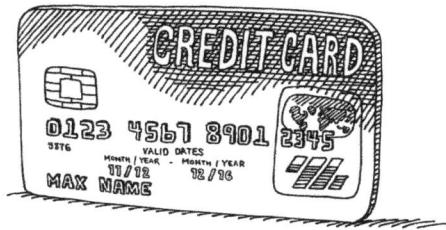

4. Ask a family member or close friend if you can borrow some cash to see you through the next couple of days.

What to do if you lose your phone

1. Try to track it down using a "find my phone" app such as *Find My iPhone* or *Wheres My Droid* (and yes, there's no apostrophe in that last one)

2. Call any recent destinations to see if they have it, and ask friends and family. Also check pockets and bags and down the sides of couches.

3. If you have no success, report it immediately to your network provider, who will block your phone. Don't worry — if you find it in the pizza box the next morning, they will usually be able to reactivate it. This is really important (not the pizza box part, the blocking part) as you will be responsible for any bills until you let your provider know.

4. If you have insurance that covers your phone, file a police report that you can then use to make a claim.

5. Even if you don't find your phone, you will need to keep paying for the contract until it runs out (yep, sad but true).

What to do if your phone stops working

1. Did you drop it in the toilet or let it get wet? Get as much water out as possible by shaking and blowing, remove batteries if you can, and then let it dry in a big bag of rice (instant rice preferably). If you're interested, look at *Water Damage Truth*[43] for a study about how effective this method is. Not very, sadly, but some people swear by it and it can't hurt so it's worth a try.

2. Did you drop it, or it got wet and the rice method failed? Go to a cell phone repair store, and cough up for repairs. A screen can cost $50 or less to repair.

3. Has it just stopped working and you are under contract or still in warranty? Contact the place where you bought it to arrange a replacement or repair.

What to do if you've been robbed

1. Do not confront a robber. Only enter your place if you are sure it's empty.

Do not confront a robber

2. Call the police at 911 or campus security, and be prepared to give them details of where you are. If you feel unsafe, sit at a neighbor's place or in your own locked car till the police arrive.

3. Do not touch anything – this is to avoid tainting the evidence.

4. Start making a list of all the things that have been stolen.

5. Call your insurance company within 24 hours, and report the burglary.

6. Being burgled can be disconcerting, so be prepared to talk with someone about it.

What to do if the power goes out in your rental

1. Check if your neighbors still have power. If everyone's power is out, you can relax as the power company will be on the job.

2. If it's just your power that's out, check your circuit breaker box for a blown fuse, which will be the one that is tripped. Flipping it back on should do the trick. If there's not a tripped fuse, call your power supply company.

3. Try to avoid opening the refrigerator or freezer as they can warm up quickly.

4. If you are going to bed with no power, make sure you have turned off the lights and other appliances; otherwise, you could get a big fright in the middle of the night when the power comes back on!

What to do if you have no water in your rental

1. Check if your neighbors have water. If everyone's water is out, wait an hour or so. If it's still not on, call your water supply company.

2. If it's just your water that's out, call your water supply company.

3. Remember that toilets don't flush without water, so be stingy with your toilet flushing (gross but practical).

4. Make sure that if you turn on faucets to test if the water is working, you turn them off again.

What to do if you have a flood at your rental

A broken pipe

1. Turn off the water supply to the house. This is often an outside lever near the water meter or a faucet.

2. Call your water supply company if the pipe is outside your house, and call a plumber if it's inside your house.

A broken appliance

1. If it's from a broken appliance such as a dishwasher or washing machine, turn off the water supply to the appliance.

2. Mop up the mess.

3. Call a friendly repair man or woman.

What to do if you have a fire

Stovetop or oven

1. If the fire is in a pan, cover it with a well-fitting lid or fire blanket. Slide the lid in from the side rather than dropping from the top to avoid burns. If the fire is in the oven or microwave, shut the door.

2. Turn the oven or burner off as long as you can do so safely.

3. Wait till everything cools down before opening the door or moving the pan.

4. If the fire gets out of control, exit the house, and call 911.

Clothing

1. Stop, drop, and roll. Cover your face with your hands.

2. If possible, get someone to throw a woolen rug over you.

3. Keep rolling till the fire goes out.

4. Treat burns by cooling in running water for 20 minutes, and seek medical advice if the burns cover a large area or are very painful.

5. Take a painkiller.

House fire

1. Escape from the house by crawling low, as that's where you'll find the least smoky air.

2. Shut doors behind you if you can to slow the movement of the fire. Remember, they can have hot door handles.

3. Call 911 once safely outside.

4. Wait outside, and don't be tempted to go back in to get any valuables.

What to do if there is a medical emergency

1. Make sure the surrounding area is safe and that you will not be in any danger by going to help. Watch out for electrical danger.

2. See if the patient is responding by gently shaking their shoulder and talking to them.

3. If there is no response, call 911 and ask for an ambulance. Stay calm, be prepared to give your location, and don't hang up till they tell you to do so.

4. Follow instructions from the operator. Their advice will include checking the patient's airways and breathing and starting CPR.

5. Keep going until the ambulance arrives or the patient recovers.

What to do if you are burned

1. Immerse the burned part in cool running water for 20 minutes .

2. Do not apply anything else, such as aloe vera, cream, or ice packs.

3. See the doctor if the burn is very painful or covers a large area.

4. Take a painkiller.

Immerse a burn in cool running water for 20 minutes

What to do if you cut yourself

1. Apply pressure to the area with a clean pad (such as a dishtowel).

2. Elevate the part above your heart, and keep calm.

3. See a doctor if you can't control the bleeding or the cut is very deep.

What to do if you are attacked

1. If your attacker is after property (such as your cell phone or wallet), give it to them.
2. If they are trying to hurt you, scream, and make a scene.
3. Make every effort to escape to a safe place. Never allow them to take you to a second location.
4. Only fight as a last resort as it can inflame the situation.
5. Once you are safe, go to the police to make a report.
6. Seek psychological support from a trusted source.

What to do if you are broke

1. Take a deep breath, and face the situation. It won't go away by itself, but with some effort, you will be able to figure it out.
2. Get advice from a financial counselor. There may be subsidized advice to be found at home or school.
3. Call the people you owe money to in order to explain the situation. Reassure them that you are willing to pay but are in a difficult position.
4. For the short term, can you sell something? Do some extra part-time work around the neighborhood?
5. Talk to your friends — they may have advice or help to offer or at least a shoulder to cry on.

Five Top Tips

1. If you have a car accident, photograph the other person's license and license plate number as well as the damage to both cars.

2. Keep a copy of your mobile phone's IMEI number. To get it, dial *#06#, look on the back of your iPhone or go to "settings" on your Android or iPhone.

3. If the power has gone out and it's time to go to bed, make sure you turn off all your lights and radio to avoid a rude awakening in the middle of the night.

4. To put out a fire in your clothes or hair, stop, drop, and roll.

5. To stop bleeding, apply pressure to the cut with a clean pad, and elevate the injured part above the heart. Keep the patient calm.

ENDNOTES

1   http://www.scamwatch.gov.au

2   http://lowfatcooking.about.com/od/healthandfitness/a/nonstickpans.htm

3   http://www.bigoven.com/recipes/leftover

4   Franklin, P. Plastic water bottles should no longer be a wasted resource, Container Recycling Institute http://www.container-recycling.org/ index.php/issues/bottledwater/275-down-the-drain

5   http://www.webmd.com/food-recipes/features/cookware-plastics-shoppers -guide-to-food-safety?page=2

6   www.bigoven.com

7   www.nerdswithknives.com

8   http://www.cdc.gov/std/stats14/adol.htm

9   U.S. Department of Health and Human Services and U.S. Department of Agriculture. 2015-2020 Dietary Guidelines for Americans. 8th Edition. December 2015. Available at http://health.gov/dietaryguidelines/2015/ guidelines/.

10   U.S. Department of Health and Human Services. 2008 Physical Activity Guidelines for Americans. Washington (DC): U.S. Department of Health and Human Services;2008. Available at: http://www.health.gov/ paguidelines.

11   Centers for Disease Control and Prevention Alcohol use and your health. Available at http://www.cdc.gov/alcohol/fact-sheets/alcohol-use.htm

12   http://www.idf.org/webdata/docs/MetSyndrome_FINAL.pdf

13   http://kidshealth.org/teen/school_jobs/college/freshman_15.html

14   https://www.nami.org/Learn-More/Mental-Health-By-the-Numbers

15 http://www.cdc.gov/std/stats14/adol.htm

16 http://www.cdc.gov/std/stats14/adol.htm

17 http://www.cancer.org/healthy/findcancerearly/cancerscreeningguidelines/american-cancer-society-guidelines-for-the-early-detection-of-cancer

18 Urology Care Foundation. Testicular Torsion. Available at: www.urologyhealth.org/urologic-conditions/testicular-torsion.

19 Available at: https://www.plannedparenthood.org.

20 Young Person's Oral Survival Guide, Australian Dental Association

21 http://darta.net.au

22 Suiter, D. Toews, M. and Ames L., Stored Product Pests in the Home. UGA Extension, 2014

23 Choe, D, Clothes Moths. Pest Notes, University of California, March 2013

24 Ellery, B. Ice in six out of ten restaurants has more bacteria than water from toilets, The Daily Mail Australia, 2013

25 http://www.safercar.gov/Safety+Ratings

26 http://newsroom.aaa.com/2015/04/annual-cost-operate-vehicle-falls-8698-finds-aaa/

27 http://www.safercar.gov/Safety+Ratings

28 Global Status Report on Road Safety 2013. World Health Organization, 2013.

29 http://www.safercar.gov/Safety+Ratings

30 Newstead, S. & D'Elias, A. An investigation into the relationship between vehicle color and crash risk. Monash University Accident Research Centre, 2007

31 http://www.kbb.com

32 www.aaa.com

33 http://drivinglaws.aaa.com/tag/title-transfer-of-ownership/

34 AAMI, Annual Road Safety Index. 2011

35 http://www.nhtsa.gov/Driving+Safety/Teen+Drivers/Teen+Drivers+-+Additional+Resources

[36] http://www.textinganddrivingsafety.com/texting-and-driving-stats

[37] http://www.petmd.com

[38] www.adoptapet.com

[39] http://www.bankwest.com.au/media-centre/financial-indicator-series/bankwest-family-pooch-index-1269940000397

[40] http://www.nyc.gov/html/bxcb10/html/home/home.shtml

[41] Kruszelnicki, Karl S. Shout while speaking on mobile ABC Science, 2014.

[42] http://www.textinganddrivingsafety.com/texting-and-driving-stats

[43] https://www.gazelle.com/thehorn/2014/05/06/gazelles-guide-water-damage-truth-rice-galaxy-everything/

Index

www.ingramcontent.com/pod-product-compliance
Lightning Source LLC
Chambersburg PA
CBHW060009050426
42448CB00012B/2672